BAD PETS

Caught in the Act!

BAD PETS

Caught in the Act!

ALLAN ZULLO

Scholastic Inc.

To Oliver and Penelope Linquist, may the love and compassion of pets forever fill their lives.

—A. Z.

ISBN 978-1-338-66239-9

10 9 8 7 6 5 4 3 2 1   21 22 23 24 25

Printed in the U.S.A. 40

First printing 2021

Book design by Cheung Tai

CONTENTS

PET PEEVES   1

THIEVES   3

RASCALS   28

INTRUDERS   50

VILLAINS   71

BONEHEADS   89

VANDALS   113

CHOWHOUNDS   129

PET PEEVES

Oh, those silly, wild pets of ours!

Whether they bark or meow, sleep in their kennels or on your bed, lick your face or perch on your shoulder, our pets—as well as their cousins in the wild—can, at times, find unbearable ways to get our goat. Have you ever scolded your cat for swiping food off your plate, your dog for chewing on your homework, or your parrot for imitating an annoying siren? No matter, we often find it *impawsible* to keep a straight face when we're reprimanding them because, well, they're just so darn goofy, funny, and lovable. Yes, they can be as stubborn as a mule or as sly as a fox. They can go hog wild and horse around. And often, they can still weasel out of trouble.

Some of their wackiest escapades have been documented in *Bad Pets: True Tales of Misbehaving Animals, Bad Pets on the Loose!, Bad Pets Save Christmas!, Bad Pets Most Wanted!, Bad to the Bone*, and *Bad Pets Hall of Shame* (all published by Scholastic). But five books can't come close to covering the idiocy, insanity, and impishness of family pets and wild animals. So this book offers another fun collection of true accounts of animal monkey business ranging from the absurd to the zany.

For example, you will read about the dog who stole a book out of a bookstore, the family cat who flooded the house, the bears who frolicked in their own pool party, the raven who stole a tourist's camera and snapped a picture, the pet donkey who gnawed on a superexpensive sports car, the cats who took unwanted spins in washing machines, and the dogs who swallowed their owners' wedding rings.

Will our pets ever stop driving us batty with their harebrained antics? Sure, when pigs fly.

THIEVES

SEEK AND HIDE

Ben Franklin was a thief?

Well, yes, if you're referring to a golden retriever with that name. Ben was caught *red-pawed* . . . err . . . red-handed stealing toys that were being gathered for a local charity. What made this crime spree so doggone wild was where he was committing these offenses—in a police station!

Ben Franklin worked as a therapy dog for the Franklin (Massachusetts) Police Department, giving comfort to crime victims by simply being cute and charming. But under that golden fur lurked a bandit who was so chill he took things easy.

During the holiday season in 2019, the police were collecting toys for the Santa Foundation, a charity that tries to make sure needy children in the community will have some presents to open on Christmas morning. The toys were being stored in a classroom at the police station.

Officers soon noticed that some of the toys were missing. Launching an investigation, the cops quickly zeroed in on a chief suspect and were stunned to discover it was one of their own—none other than Ben Franklin, their trusted therapy dog.

They spotted him sneaking into the open room where he snatched a baby doll in its little carrier. Using his mouth to pick up the carrier by the handle, Ben trotted out of the room with the doll. When he realized that officers had spotted him, Ben scurried down the hall and into an office where he hid on his bed, which was under a desk.

But the cops were right on his tail. In fact, they recorded his attempted getaway. In the video, which the department posted on Facebook, an officer sweetly asks Ben, "Hey, where are you going with that?" The dog turns, steals a glance at the cop, and then continues on his way. Another officer breaks into laughter and tells Ben, "Oh, you're priceless." When they peer under the desk, they find the booty he had stolen—several plush animals. "He's going to keep stockpiling toys if he keeps bringing them in here," the second officer says.

Later, Deputy Chief James Mill explained to Boston TV station WFXT, "When Ben saw the toys, he thought they all belonged to him."

Although they recovered the toys, officers couldn't donate them to the needy children because the stolen items were covered in Ben's slobber, so they were replaced.

The crafty dog didn't get a charge out of stealing because officials declined to prosecute him. However, he was banned from the room that held the toys.

"We learned an extremely valuable lesson today," the department said on the Facebook post, which included video of Ben's latest heist. "When you have a classroom full of toys ready to be shipped off to the Santa Foundation, you should: 1. Close the door to the classroom or 2. Keep the toys elevated." The department added that it had to take these precautions because if not, the golden retriever would slowly swipe the toys throughout the day and bring them back to his lair.

No one was mad at Ben. "He has the run of the station," said Mill. "It's amazing. He's like that guy who shows up to the party that everyone loves. Seriously, if Ben walks in, it's like a ray of sunshine."

Ben might have been inspired by another in-house thief—a four-year-old Labrador retriever mix named Kevin.

After his previous owner no longer could care for him and dropped him off at the Austin (Texas) Animal Center in 2019, Kevin appeared to be quite sweet. But that was all a *dog and phony* show. He was as crooked as a hound's hind leg, swiping things every chance he got—a blanket, toys, spare change, clothing, and even a woman's purse.

The no-kill animal shelter was so overcrowded and short of kennels that some of the good-natured dogs who were up for adoption, like Kevin, were kept in offices. That was the perfect opportunity for him to use his stealthy skills, sneaking around various offices and walking off with stolen goods. He'd bring his loot back to his bed, which was underneath a desk.

"Every time that I've been assigned to take care of the office dogs, I'll go in there and I'll notice his pile happens to be a little bit bigger than the last time I was in there," animal care worker Caitlyn Kretsinger told Austin TV station KXAN. She said an employee had taken off her sweater and draped it over a chair, but when she returned, it was gone. She had a good idea about where it was. "It was underneath Kevin and he was snoozing on it," Kretsinger said.

Shelter workers were very understanding, Jennifer Olohan, AAC's communications and media manager, told KXAN. "He doesn't really have a whole lot, you know," she said in 2019 after Kevin had been there for four months. "He's got a couple toys, he's got his food bowl, and he's got his bed, but that's really all he has."

The tendency to steal is probably rooted in the absence of people who he once knew, she added. "I think he's trying the best he can to maintain that presence by taking our stuff. It makes him feel closer to us. It's kind of sweet and endearing—even if you are the person who's lost your shirt."

EASY MONEY

For years, Theo the cat was notorious for stealing items from neighbors' houses and yards and bringing his booty home. But then he upped his game. He stole money.

Theo pulled off the crime shortly after his owners, Rachael Drouet and Paul Edwards, moved into a new residence in Ipswich, Suffolk, England, in 2019. He strutted into the house carrying a plastic bag containing the equivalent of $32 in cash.

Fortunately, there was a note inside with an address, so the couple was able to learn that a neighbor had left the money outside his front door for the milkman. Edwards returned the cash, apologized, and explained that Theo was an "ASBO cat." ASBO is a British term referring to a court order given to someone displaying antisocial behavior.

"The young lad smiled, took the money, and acted like that kind of thing happened all the time," Edwards told the BBC. "It's been a great way for me to introduce our cat's behavior to the new neighbors.

"Stern words [were] had with Theo. Mistake pointed out, he was full of apologies."

The nine-year-old black-and-white Siamese turned to a life of crime when he was three in 2013. He began snatching Christmas decorations from neighbors' trees and bringing them home. Then, playing a devious game of *cat-and-house*, he sneaked through doggy doors and swiped such items as a phone charger, a hand puppet, a pen, and even a child's artwork. Theo loved pilfering the toys belonging to other felines. *Curiosity thrilled the cat.*

"We sheepishly had to go to our neighbors with a handful of cat toys," Edwards told the BBC at the time.

He said one of the neighbors had young twins who invited Theo into their home because they liked him. "He started stealing things from them, and it kind of went downhill from there," Edwards said. Drouet recalled that Theo broke into the twins' house, "ran upstairs, and nicked [stole] a fluffy pink pen from their bedroom right in front of them. Luckily, they thought it was hilarious."

Theo fancied himself as the cat's meow. Drouet said Theo had turned into "a bit of a neighborhood celebrity for all the wrong reasons." Then she joked, "We live in hope that one day he'll bring back an iPad or something of significant value."

Prime time was crime time for Theo when he would do his nightly cat walk. He just couldn't restrain himself from stealing, prompting his owners to go on Facebook in 2015 and apologize after he had brought home plastic toy food, including an eggplant, pineapple, green pepper, cheese, fish, and the felt basket that held them. The Facebook post also featured a photo of Theo's biggest heist to date—a child's blue hooded quilted vest.

Earlier in the year, Theo stole a catalog from a house down the street owned by a police officer, which Drouet admitted, "wasn't ideal."

The couple managed to return the stolen items to their rightful owners. Added Drouet, "You get tired of knocking on neighbors' doors and saying, 'Me again.'"

She said she thought that moving to a new neighborhood in 2019 would curb the cat's lust for loot. At first, he behaved. But he simply couldn't resist stealing the milk money. "We are deeply ashamed of our cat," Drouet said, "especially as he had convinced us that he had changed his criminal ways."

One thing you can say about Theo: He's got *cattitude*.

RUFF RIDE

Elvis, a 13-year-old black Labrador retriever, found a way to drive his owner bonkers—by stealing the man's pickup truck.

His master, Paul Shearn, of Owensboro, Kentucky, packed up his truck to spend a camping weekend in 2018 on his grandfather's farm. Among the things he brought were camping gear, a fishing rod and equipment, a cast-iron skillet, and a container of bacon grease. Oh, and his trusty four-legged sidekick, Elvis, of course.

On the way, Shearn stopped off at a Meijer Supercenter to pick up some fresh ground beef for grilling burgers over a campfire. Because it was a warm day, he left the truck running with the air conditioning on so Elvis would stay cool.

"I said, 'Elvis, don't go acting a fool and get people calling the cops on us,'" Shearn recalled in an interview with the *Owensboro Times*.

While Shearn was in the store, Elvis thought if he was ever going to drive a truck, it's now or never. Getting behind the wheel, the dog knocked the gear selector into drive, and the truck rolled forward across the parking lot and stopped when it struck a parked car belonging to store employee David Adams.

When someone told Adams about the accident, he

ran out to the parking lot and saw the dog in the front seat. Elvis was not all shook up. "The dog was all calm, not barking, and acting like it was no big deal," Adams told the newspaper.

When Shearn came out of the store, he spotted a police car at the scene of the mishap. "I wondered what idiot would park his truck so close to another car." It took him only a few seconds to realize that it was his own truck that had hit the parked car—and that Elvis was a canine devil in disguise.

Suspicious minds figured out what had happened. Shearn had left the container of bacon grease on the dashboard. That was just way too tempting for Elvis because, like most dogs, he had a burning love for bacon. In his quest for the treat, he had engaged the truck into drive and merrily watched as it slowly banged into Adams's car. All he could do after that was surrender.

Fortunately, Elvis wasn't hurt. Although Shearn's truck wasn't damaged, the driver's side rear panel of Adams's car was dented. Shearn, a youth pastor at Christ Community Church, said he, Adams, and the police officer who investigated the mishap shared a good laugh. "I don't know what God's plan is in all of this," Shearn said. "Maybe it's that everyone needs a little more laughter."

The officer didn't ticket Shearn, and Shearn didn't punish Elvis, who was probably thinking, "Don't be cruel."

Actually, it was quite the opposite. Said Shearn, "That's all right."

Another pet dog, a mutt named Duke, took his owner's car for an *oy!* ride in 2019.

Duke was left alone in his master's gold 2001 Mercedes-Benz S430, which was parked on a slight hill in a residential area of Aptos, California. As Duke moved from the passenger seat to the driver's side, his leash became tangled with the car's gear shift, and he yanked it into neutral. And that's when he met some neighbors by accident.

With Duke directly behind the steering wheel, the car began rolling backward down the street. Neighbors Jim and Janie Black told San Francisco TV station KPIX they stared in disbelief as Duke drove home the point that he was a terrible motorist. The Mercedes-Benz slammed into their two garbage cans, ran over their mailbox, and crashed into their retaining wall, knocking over dozens of bricks before it came to a halt.

The Blacks rushed over to the car and saw Duke, who was unhurt and still sitting behind the steering wheel, looking back at them with a boy-that-was-fun expression. The couple took photos of the car thief, which went viral on social media. As for Duke's owner, he planned *to steer his dog away from ever braking bad* again.

PORCH PIRATES

Packages that delivery people leave by the front door sometimes get snatched by box bandits. But the culprits aren't always human. Take, for example, a Great Pyrenees named Max. He was a big, goofy beast who enjoyed playing with the neighbor's grandchildren. Little did they know that he was also a sneaky thief.

Around Christmastime in 2019, the kids' grandmother, Debbie Goines, of Shady Point, Oklahoma, was expecting a holiday package from her sister-in-law in California. The box contained Christmas treats, special kinds of beef jerky and olive oil. Goines received a notice that the shipment had arrived and was left on the front porch. However, when she opened the front door, the package wasn't there. "I thought, 'Good grief, maybe the wind carried it off or something,'" she told Fort Smith, Arkansas, TV station KHBS. "We were really puzzled."

Goines had a camera on her doorbell, so she checked the video, which clearly showed that a thief had come up to her front door and walked off with her package. But this was no ordinary porch pirate. No, this was a pooch pirate—none other than the friendly Max. "He just politely picked up the package and carried it home," Goines said. "I guess he smelled the jerky and thought that it had been delivered to the wrong house."

Goines called the dog's owner and told him about Max's crime. A search of the area turned up the package, or what was left of it. The box was destroyed and most of its contents were gone. "All my neighbor found was an empty box and a busted bottle of olive oil," Goines said. "I assumed Max ate what he wanted and buried the rest."

After putting the fluffy white pet in doggy detention in his kennel, the embarrassed neighbor apologized to Goines and offered to pay for all the lost goodies. But Goines declined the offer. "There are no hard feelings," she said. "Max is still welcome to play in my yard with my grandchildren."

For Max, Christmas was still the most *plunderful* time of the year.

A young bear wanted some takeout food, so he took it—right off the front porch of a family's house.

Aidan Newman of Thornhurst Township, Pennsylvania, said when he came home one afternoon in 2019, he spotted a young bear in the yard. Seeing a human, the bear scooted off into the woods. Newman and his girlfriend went inside, momentarily ignoring six boxes that a delivery driver had dropped off earlier in the day. The largest box contained dog food and treats from the mail-order company Chewy for his dogs Cleo, a golden retriever, and Bella, a St. Bernard.

Several minutes later, Newman went onto the porch to bring in the boxes. They were all there except for the one from Chewy. From the porch, Newman scanned the yard and saw that the bear was just inside the tree line munching contentedly on the dog food.

Newman checked the video from a home security camera and watched with a mixture of amusement and amazement as the bear cautiously climbs the stairs to the front porch. Zeroing in on only the Chewy box, which is about half the bear's size, the culprit chomps on a corner and drags the package down the steps. Without letting go, the bad bruin lugs the box across the yard and into the woods where he enjoys a feast.

"I thought it was funny, and I thought it was cute, too," Newman told Scranton, Pennsylvania, TV station WNEP. "I have never seen a bear do that before, so it was pretty crazy that we caught it on camera."

Smarter than the average bear, the bruin apparently was casing the house and ready to pull off the theft earlier but then backed away when Newman showed up. "After my girlfriend and I went in the house, the bear came back onto the porch and ran off with the Chewy box," Newman said. "Later when we went outside, we saw him hiding in the box, chilling in the shade and munching on the dog food."

Although Newman and his family found the whole thing hilarious, Cleo and Bella were not amused. However, when Newman emailed Chewy a copy of the video showing the crime, the company sent his pets a new box of dog food. This time, Newman immediately brought the package into the house. He knew that somewhere out there, a dog food–loving bruin considered another Chewy box a *bear necessity*.

WISH BOOK

A homeless dog ambled into a college bookstore, snatched a book off a shelf, and left with it. But he didn't get far before he was collared. However, out of his misdeed came a good deed—one that led to a new chapter in the life of the four-legged book thief.

The skinny brown mutt had been hanging around outside the Feevale University bookstore in Novo Hamburgo, Brazil, for several days in 2018. No one paid the cute brown stray any attention until one day he acted as though he wanted the world to know about his sad plight.

As security video shows, he walks through the open door of the store and, without anyone noticing him, heads to a display of books near the front. Sniffing around the bottom shelf, he picks out a specific book, and then, wagging his tail while gripping the book with his teeth, he leaves the store.

But that's hardly the end of the story.

Moments after his getaway, the canine shoplifter was stopped by a student. There was no fight in this dog, so he dropped the book, which the student picked up and returned to the clerk who was working the front desk. When they looked at the title, they were stunned. Of all the books he could have chosen to steal, he picked out a novel that described him the best. It was called *The Days of Abandonment*.

The staff at the store, whose hearts the canine thief had stolen, posted video of his novel heist on Facebook, and it soon went viral.

But that's still not the end of the story. Two volunteers from the Amparo Animal Project saw the video and rushed to the university where they found the shoplifter. They took him to a shelter where he was given a bath, medication, and vaccinations and then placed in a foster family. Because he was so skinny, he was nicknamed Kustelinha, a play off the Portuguese word *costelinha*, which means *ribs*.

After Kustelinha was nursed back to health, he was

handed over to his forever home where his saga finally had a happy ending.

GRIN AND BARE IT

Two pet dogs turned into thieving big mouths when they stole—and wore—human false teeth.

Maggie, a Shih Tzu/poodle/Chihuahua mix, lived with her owner, Eunice (who declined to give her last name), and Eunice's parents on Long Island, New York. Her father would watch the dog while Eunice was at work.

"My dad decided to take an afternoon nap and rather than put his dentures in the bathroom, he left them on a napkin on the end of the couch," Eunice told BuzzFeed in 2018. "While he was sleeping, Maggie jumped up and grabbed them."

After Eunice's father woke up, he noticed that his false teeth were missing. During his search, he found the reason why: Maggie was hiding under the living room table wearing his dentures. After taking several photos of the culprit giving a false impression that she had grown human teeth, he retrieved his choppers, which, fortunately, weren't damaged.

Eunice said that her father then texted her about the

false (teeth) alarm. "I was in tears laughing and showing all of my coworkers," she told BuzzFeed. After she posted photos of Maggie's hilarious smile on Twitter, they went viral, and now Maggie has an Instagram page dedicated to her antics. Apparently, snatching the man's dentures didn't leave a bad taste in her mouth.

A year later, Luna, a mischievous mutt rescued off the streets by a loving family, proved that she, too, was armed to the teeth.

She lived with her owner, Anna Carolina Lima, of Minas Gerais, Brazil. Early one afternoon while dog-sitting Luna, Lima's grandmother lay down to take her daily nap. Like always, she removed her dentures and placed them beneath her pillow, and then went to sleep. When she woke up, the woman reached for her false teeth, but they weren't there. She looked in the pillowcases and sheets and under the bed. She couldn't find them anywhere, even after Lima returned home and helped with the search. Losing one's teeth would really suck.

Lima told local reporters that she suspected Luna had stolen the dentures. "She is very clever," Lima said. "She picks things up and hides them. Hours later, Luna was playing around the house in the darkness, and when

I called, she came to me with a cute face and her tail wagging, jumping around. But she did not have the dentures.

"Later on, I found Luna on the sofa with the teeth in her mouth." Having discovered them by the *grin of her teeth*, Lima snapped several photos of Luna baring Grandma's choppers. When Lima tried to retrieve them, the dog gritted her teeth and refused to give them up.

"I was eventually able to distract her and take them away," Lima said. "Luckily, they weren't damaged."

Lima, who posted the photos on social media, said neither she nor her grandmother could stay mad at Luna. "We love animals," she said. "Even naughty ones."

BOO BIRD

Like a sneaky pickpocket, a crafty seagull swiped a wallet containing a man's money and credit cards right out of his beach bag.

The theft happened at Singing Beach in Manchester-by-the-Sea, Massachusetts. Aaron Weiner of nearby Beverly had taken his family there for an after-dinner swim one summer evening in 2018. He put his belongings, including his wallet, in a beach bag. But he failed to zip it up—an oversight noticed by the cunning seagull, whose species is known for mugging people of their ice-cream cones, French fries, and sandwiches.

"We were enjoying a nice evening at the beach, and had been there for like an hour," Weiner told Boston TV station WBZ. "All of a sudden a guy came running up saying that a bird had stolen my wallet. And I thought he was a lunatic."

Other witnesses confirmed the *fowl* play to Weiner. He said the bird fished his wallet out of the beach bag and got away with $200, his credit cards, and his driver's license. Thinking the feathered fiend was still around or had dropped the wallet, Weiner and his wife scoured the area in the hope that the bird would show them the money. But because the sun was setting and it was getting dark, they called off the search.

"On the way home, we called the police," Weiner said. "They were in disbelief that a seagull had taken my wallet."

Scott Santino of Mass Audubon, a conservation education organization, said seagulls are notorious thieves. "Coastal habitats are where seagulls forage for food," he told WBZ. Santino said the gull probably thought Weiner's shiny money clip was a crab. "It's best to keep your belongings out of sight while swimming," he added.

Weiner learned his lesson. When he returned to the beach two days later, he put his things back in the same beach bag in the same pocket as before. "But I zipped it up this time."

He never found his wallet and figured, if money talks, it had said, "Goodbye."

DOWN IN THE DUMPS

A bear nicknamed Cheeseburger took out the trash from a local store. But he wasn't trying to be nice. He literally took out the trash—by stealing the dumpster.

For a few weeks in 2019, the large black bear had been seen on security cameras hanging around at night behind a store in Lyons, Colorado. Employees at the store had spotted him about ten times trying to forage through garbage cans and bins in the area. They began calling him Cheeseburger because he had scored some discarded fast food.

Desperately wanting to dumpster dive behind the store, the bear burst through the gate of a locked wooden fence that surrounded the large metal trash container in the back.

"As soon as the doors [of the gate] blew open, I thought, 'This is something out of a horror film,'" store manager Nikko Garza told Denver TV station KDVR when describing what he saw on the store's security video later. Referring to a creepy Stephen King movie in which the main character tries to break into a locked bathroom by chopping the door with an ax, Garza said Cheeseburger "busted through like in *The Shining*." Ironically, several scenes from the film were shot at the nearby Stanley Hotel.

Try as he might, Cheeseburger couldn't open the bear-proof lid, much to his frustration.

But the bear refused to give up. Even though the trash bin contained nothing but smashed boxes, according to Garza, the bear sensed there were some worthwhile goodies inside it.

In the video, which Colorado Parks and Wildlife posted on social media, Cheeseburger stands up on his hind legs and, grasping the dumpster with his front paws, drags the heavy wheeled bin out of the fenced-in area and through the busted gate while walking backward. Once he clears the fence, the bear then pushes the dumpster down an alleyway out of camera range to a nearby parking lot. Still unable to open the lid, Cheeseburger finally abandons the bin.

Garza said he wasn't sure if the bear was planning on bringing the dumpster home to his den, but at least "he was showing some initiative." However, Cheeseburger likely decided that scrounging for high-calorie garbage was a complete waste of time.

TAKING THEIR SWEET TIME

Thieving squirrels have been hanging around the bars—candy bars, that is. During a two-year crime spree, at least two of the furry rodents were sneaking into a Toronto, Canada, convenience store and stealing sweet treats right off the shelves.

"I always see them sneaking outside the door, looking in my store, and even right at me," Paul Kim, owner of Luke's Grocery and Snack Bar, told the *Toronto Star* in 2017. Referring to candy bars popular in Canada, he said, "They come in and take a Crunchie, Crispy Crunch, Wunderbar or even try to take a Mr. Big."

Like taking candy from a baby, the two pesky squirrels—one black, one gray—were making almost daily theft attempts in 2016. "I think we've lost up to 48 candy bars this fall season," Kim's daughter Cindy told the newspaper. "That's an extremely rough estimate, though, because we have no way of knowing when we've been robbed. They're very sneaky.

"We find them very, very cute. However, these squirrels have stolen considerably from us this fall, so we'd like that to stop."

The squirrels struck whenever the door to the store was left open for up to an hour for cleaning, restocking, or letting in fresh air. "When the door is open and we're not around for a moment, they sneak in," Cindy told the *Star*. "They've yet to fail."

She posted video on social media of the squirrely criminals scurrying out of the store with candy bars in their mouths. One post shows a crime committed by each squirrel. In the first one, the gray squirrel inches tentatively into the store, then hurries over to the lowest shelf containing candy bars and snatches a $2 Kinder Bueno before scampering out the door and across the street. The second video shows the black squirrel duplicating the theft, only this time it was a $1.80 Crunchie bar.

In a Reddit post asking for suggestions on how to stop the nutty squirrels, Cindy wrote:

"Though we can't see [the squirrel] the moment it commits the theft because the candy bars are displayed below the counter on the customer's side, we can hear a distinct rustling. When we come around the counter to try to catch the squirrel, we can see it running off with the bar in its mouth. We tried running after [the squirrel], but it's still faster. A couple times, [passersby] and customers tried chasing after it with us, but once [the squirrel] goes up a tree, it's game over."

Reddit users suggested the Kims use a screen door or owl decoys or spread red pepper on the shelves. The only thing that seemed to work was the onset of winter, when the squirrels were stopped cold in their tracks.

*　　*　　*

A squirrel turned into the Grinch Who Stole Christmas during the holidays in 2017.

The rodent was videoed stealing outdoor Christmas lights from the home of Margaret Rican of Seattle, Washington. It wasn't just a few or a few dozen. No, this rascal scampered off with more than 150 bulbs, swiping them one at a time. Pulling up to red lights, getting the green lights, and failing to slow down for yellow lights, he was clever enough to remove each light off the strand and scamper into the neighbor's yard.

"He's a little squirrel that we are calling the Bulb Bandit," Rican wrote on YouTube, which featured a brief clip of the thief running off with a yellow bulb. "We want to believe that this little varmint is decorating his nest. But, really, we think that he believes these to be food. He has stolen 150 in 24 hours, carefully and precisely chewing through the wires to steal the bulbs and bury them around the neighborhood."

At first, Rican was annoyed by the holiday thefts because she faced a dim outlook, so she tried to put a stop to them. She placed nuts out on her deck, hoping the *light-headed* squirrel would take them instead of the bulbs. She even sprinkled cayenne pepper near the lights to discourage the crook. But nothing worked. Rican finally gave up and came to admire the culprit's work ethic.

"He's the hardest working rodent we've ever seen, and we are really pulling for him, and hoping he survives this winter," Rican said. "He's a quick little bandit, with really good hops." To the squirrel, the thefts must have seemed de-*lightful*.

RASCALS

FOOTLOOSE AND FANCY FREE

When it comes to escape artists, Quilty the tabby was in a class by himself. Not only could he repeatedly break out of his room at an animal shelter, but he often triggered chaos by setting his feline friends free as well.

The striped rascal was born at the Friends for Life Animal Rescue and Adoption center in Houston, Texas, in 2012 and was eventually adopted out. Staffers assumed that was the last they would see of him. But in 2019, he was returned to the shelter because his owner was moving and couldn't bring him along.

Shelter workers weren't aware that the cute lovable cat had the soul of a sly fox. At his adoptive home, he had perfected the art of opening a closed door by jumping up and grabbing the handle with his paws. The *cath-letic* Quilty would hang on the handle just long enough to yank it down and spring open the door, allowing the family dog to sneak out of the house.

When Quilty arrived at the shelter, he was eventually placed in one of its "free roam" rooms where more than a dozen senior cats lived together rather than in individual kennels. But to Quilty, "free roam" meant that a cat should be free to roam wherever and whenever it wanted.

Days after his arrival, staffers showed up one morning to find Quilty and the other senior cats frolicking in the hallways and lobby. The workers assumed that someone had forgotten to properly close the door to the senior room. But then it happened again and again.

"We would arrive in the morning and have to collect all fifteen cats, who had had a blast during the night," Jennifer Hopkins, the spokeswoman for Friends for Life, told CNN. Employees studied surveillance video and discovered the culprit responsible for the mass breakouts was that conniving, crafty cat Quilty. In the video, he uses the same technique that he did at his adoptive home. But in this case, when the door swings open, he and the other cats scurry out of the room.

Staffers were forced to "Quilty-proof" the senior room. The door opened inward, so they placed a broomstick-like bar horizontally across the door's exterior and attached it by rope to the outside handle so when Quilty pulled on the inside handle, the bar would prevent the door from opening. But they agreed their best option to prevent further escapes was to get the cunning cat adopted out. So they turned to their Facebook page and posted photos of him with the comment:

"Quilty will not be contained. And he has no shame. Quilty loves to let cats out of the senior room. Repeatedly. We have since Quilty-proofed the cat room, while he took a brief hiatus [break] in the lobby. His roommates missed him while he was banished to the lobby. They enjoyed their nighttime escapades around the shelter. The staff, however, did not miss the morning cat wrangling, so we'll just have to agree to disagree there . . . If someone out there is looking for a clever cat that gets along with dogs but does not get along with closed doors, we have someone they really need to come and meet. Please. Come meet him. And take him home. Please . . ."

Before he could be returned to the senior room, he had to spend some time in an "integration kennel" so that he could readjust to his surroundings. The shelter posted photos of Quilty by the glass door expressing his extreme annoyance. He was a real sourpuss. "THE DISPLEASURE!" read the caption. "He is being a spicy [jerk] now because he is, once again, contained . . ."

Ah, but not for long. The wily feline *purr*severed and managed to escape again, prompting this Facebook post: "Quilty's review with the parole board was denied, so he released himself of his own recognizance today. He felt that confinement had nothing more to offer him. He has been returned to solitary. The review board will take up his case again tomorrow."

After he was allowed back into the senior room, he still managed to slip out several times by timing his breakout when a staffer opened the door to enter the room. One time, the Houdini-like cat made a wrong turn and ended up crashing a staff meeting. The shelter posted a brief video of Quilty being returned to his confines. "This [jerk] got out. We perp-walked him back to the room. We cannot wait for him to go on his sleepover with his potential adopter. Like . . . cannot frickin' wait."

The frequent social media updates about Quilty's escapades turned him into an Internet star with tens of thousands of followers. Trying to cash in on his celebrity status, the shelter began selling FREE QUILTY T-shirts and rubber bracelets.

The cat even got a special shout-out on Comedy Central's *The Daily Show with Trevor Noah*. On the show, comedian Roy Wood Jr. cracked, "Good luck to any family that adopts Quilty. The parents are going to come home and look around the house, and they're going to be like, 'Hey! Who opened the baby gate?' Quilty's going to be like, 'Hey, I don't believe that kids should be in cages.'"

All the attention paid off for Quilty. He was finally adopted out to a family with two dogs. In a Facebook update, his new owner said, "He has really taken over the role of King of the house. He loves to be held like a baby and have his tummy rubbed . . . He has us all wrapped around his paws for sure! Anytime he is ignored, he just starts meowing REALLY loudly and then, Bam, he is being loved on and spoiled . . . He definitely has us all doing his bidding and goes to whomever he thinks will give him the most treats."

In response, the shelter commented, "BELLY RUBS? WHO EVEN ARE YOU ANYMORE, QUILTY?"

HAPPY MEALS

Princess the pit bull mix repeatedly pulled off a clever canine con that kept her fat cells happy.

The dog would sneak out of the house at night, trot over to the nearby McDonald's, and, while pretending to be a homeless pooch, beg for food. The scam worked great until the *hamburglar* was busted by her owner.

In 2018, Betsy Reyes of Oklahoma City couldn't figure out why Princess had unexpectedly been gaining weight, even though she was on the same diet and getting the same amount of exercise as usual. Because Princess started leaving the yard at night, Reyes decided to tail her one evening.

To her surprise, Reyes spotted Princess beside the McDonald's drive-through lane, acting like a hungry, abandoned, down-on-her-luck stray. Gazing up at the drivers with her forlorn puppy dog eyes, she silently pleaded for them to toss her their just-purchased hamburgers. Oh, she was good because people were falling for her homeless act. Princess was hoping for *burger and better things*.

Reyes used her phone to record a driver taking the hamburger out of the bun and tossing it to Princess, who polished it off in a mega-bite. That was all Reyes had to see. She *mustard* the ability to *ketchup* to her dog.

Steering her car in the drive-through lane, she waited until Princess trotted over and began the woe-is-me performance. Reyes rolled down the window and then scolded the dog. When Princess realized the jig was up, she turned away from Reyes—and then tried (unsuccessfully) to scam another driver. It was *food for naught*. She reluctantly got into her owner's car.

Reyes then went on Facebook and dog-shamed Princess. Accompanying video and photos of Princess's last successful con, Reyes wrote, "If you see my dog @ the McDonald's on Shields [Boulevard], quit feeding her . . . She's not even a stray dog. She's just a gold diggin' [dog] acting like she's a stray so people will feel bad for her & feed her burgers."

The post went viral, prompting one person to comment: "I know the same dog here . . . and, yes, she made me feed her, and then I saw her walking home."

SOUNDING THE ALARM

The fun-loving ways of Jazz, an African gray parrot, alarmed not only his owner but firefighters, too. He sent everyone into emergency mode by his remarkably good impression of a blaring smoke detector.

Steve Dockerty of Daventry, Northamptonshire, England, had adopted the 17-year-old bird a year earlier as a companion for his pet parrot, Kiki. The two feathered friends got along great and enjoyed mimicking sounds and voices.

But Jazz outdid himself one afternoon in 2018 after the smoke alarm went off in Dockerty's home. For no apparent reason, the device would occasionally screech on its own even when there was no fire. That was the case this time after Dockerty made a quick check around the residence.

Because the alarm was monitored by a security company, Dockerty received a call from one of its operators asking if everything was all right. He assured the caller that there was no fire. However, Dockerty found it strange that even though he had turned off the alarm, it began to shriek again. He didn't realize that the operator, who also heard the alarm in the background during the conversation, thought the same thing.

After hanging up, the operator—trying to err on the side of safety—alerted the Northamptonshire Fire and Rescue Service, which rushed firefighters to the house. Banging on the door, they asked Dockerty to point out the fire. He explained there was no fire although everyone could clearly hear the alarm.

"The fire crew were a bit confused to say the least," Dockerty told the British newspaper *Metro*. He said they went throughout the house and examined and cleaned the smoke detectors, but the blaring continued. "Then we heard the noise coming from Jazz and that's how we figured out it was him," Dockerty said. "He's a cheeky sod [rascal] and likes to imitate things. He imitated the smoke alarm so well he fooled all of us, including the fire brigade." When Jazz stopped doing his impression from the comfort of his cage, "he was laughing his socks offs," his owner said.

Northamptonshire Fire and Rescue Watch Commander Norman James told *Metro*, "It certainly made the crew smile and although it was a false alarm, we are thankful there was no actual fire and that the homeowner and his two parrots were safe."

Said Dockerty, "The fire crew were very good about it and even came around the next day to check if the birds were okay. The birds will literally imitate anything to get my attention. That was the first time either of the two birds had ever imitated the fire alarm though.

"They tend to make noises when I'm out of the room. Every day there is something new with them. They'll be getting me in more mischief sometime in the future, that's for sure." Well, having a parrot says a lot about the owner.

PRANK YOU VERY MUCH

In a literally open-and-shut case, Sizzle the pug was found guilty of pulling off a dirty trick on his sister Elphie.

The prankster—who was named after NFL All-Pro defensive end Terrell "T-Sizzle" Suggs—was adopted by Andrew and Michelle Nechetsky from the Delaware Valley Pug Rescue in Avondale, Pennsylvania. He and

Elphie, also a pug, were exceptionally close and were *mutts* about each other.

In fact, Elphie, who had been a part of the couple's family for more than a year, hated being separated from her adopted little brother. Because Sizzle was a puppy, he was kept in a crate in the kitchen when the couple went to work. "We would put a gate in between the kitchen and the hallway so Elphie wouldn't bother him while we were gone," Nechetsky told thedodo.com in 2020.

But more than once, when the Nechetskys came home, they would find their two pugs roaming around outside Sizzle's kennel. At first the couple wondered if Michelle had forgotten to latch the gate and the crate. But that seemed like a *re-pug-nant* idea.

They soon discovered that Elphie was the one responsible for the crate escape. Despite her size, Elphie was able to climb over the gate and into the kitchen, where Sizzle was in his kennel. Even more remarkable, she was able to figure out how to unlatch the crate's door with her nose to spring Sizzle.

Because the dogs hadn't caused any trouble when they were roaming the residence, the Nechetskys stopped locking up Sizzle when the couple left for work.

You would think that Sizzle would have been extra nice to his big sister for gaining his freedom, but nooooo.

As a thank-you, he pulled off a practical joke that caused her to lose *her* freedom.

More than once, the Nechetskys returned home to face an unexpected and, at first, an unexplained puzzle: Elphie was locked in Sizzle's kennel. But how could that be? The couple was perplexed because there was no way Elphie could have wandered into the crate and locked herself in. The latch was on the outside of the door. Home security cameras weren't angled right to provide an answer.

"I started coming home from work and I'd open the front door and hear her crying," Andrew told thedodo.com. "I'd walk into the kitchen and see her locked in the crate. I honestly couldn't for the life of me figure out how she got in there."

The real cause escaped the couple at first. Then, one day, Sizzle trotted into the kitchen. "I saw him open the crate, then he walked away, grabbed a little pig toy, and put it in the crate," Andrew recalled. "He walked away and waited. She went looking for her pig, saw it in the crate, walked in, and sat next to it. Then he closed the door and used his mouth to latch it shut. It blew my freakin' mind." Meanwhile, Sizzle just sauntered off as if nothing had happened. Andrew quickly let Elphie out of the kennel.

There's an old saying: "Fool me once, shame on you. Fool me twice, shame on me." Well, Sizzle tried the same prank again a few hours later—and Elphie fell for it again. Only this time, Andrew recorded it.

Sizzle didn't have any more opportunities for his clever trick because the Nechetskys got rid of the crate. The couple believe Sizzle wasn't being mean to his sister. "I think he did it as a game," Andrew said. "He loves to play with her and they get along great. Every day I come home now, they're cuddling on the couch. These pups are the best—even when they're bad."

BLESS YOU

A stray cat did her best to interrupt a religious service at a Buddhist temple, but she didn't have a prayer.

Nevertheless, her antics, which were videoed, ended up being a blessing for hundreds of thousands of Internet viewers.

To honor the new year in 2020, several Buddhist monks at the Wat Udomrangsi temple on the outskirts of Bangkok, Thailand, sat cross-legged on a stage in a five-hour-long prayer vigil. The Thai temple, like so many others, is the home of about a dozen stray cats who are fed by animal lovers. The felines seldom cause any problems for the monks, whose religion teaches them to respect all living things.

Respect is one thing; patience is another, which is what one of the monks displayed in abundance when a persistent but lovable cat chose the prayer vigil to demand some cuddle time. While monk Luang Pi Komkrit Taechachoto, 25, had his hands clasped in prayer and was chanting with his fellow monks, the light brown cat hopped onto his lap and began kneading his right thigh. Komkrit kept chanting, but when the cat started pawing on his arm, the monk gently tried to *whisker* away.

The cat refused to take the hint. The glamour puss walked across his saffron-colored robe and began rubbing her face against his left forearm. Unable to get his full attention, she went back across his lap and gave a little head bump to his hands. The monk could no longer keep a straight face. He cracked a smile and gave her a few pats.

His gesture hardly satisfied her, and she began kneading his right shoulder and then his chest, blocking the view of his scripture book. Her demand for some loving caught the eye of an older monk seated next to Komkrit. The senior monk at first flashed a stern look at the cat, but he didn't throw a *temple tantrum*. In fact, his expression quickly turned into a smirk. As for Komkrit, he could no longer ignore her and began petting the cat, which was exactly what she wanted all along.

"I was trying to read the book," Komkrit told Reuters news agency. "But I was more focused on the cat."

Nophayong Sookphan, who took the video, told Reuters the cat leaped onto the stage at about 15 minutes to midnight and wouldn't leave until after the New Year's Day countdown. When the video was posted on social media, it went viral and was even shown on Thai TV.

So did that cat stop trying to interrupt other prayer vigils by the monks? *Fat chants.*

(E)SCAPEGOAT

If Lancelot the billy goat could talk, he would say he was just horsing around. In a way, he was. He cleverly unlocked a gate, allowing two of his buddies—both huge Clydesdales—to escape. One of the fugitives remained on the loose for five days.

Lancelot, a Nigerian dwarf, lived with his horse pals Buddy and Harry on a ranch near Santa Cruz, California. Despite their difference in size, the one-ton horses enjoyed hanging around the frisky little goat inside their locked pen. Although the Clydesdales appreciated all the love and *horsepitality* that their owner, Tamara Schmitz, gave them, they had a streak of wanderlust in them. They were always looking for a chance to see just how green the grass was on the other side of the fence.

To escape, they needed Lancelot's help, and he provided it one evening in 2016. "I closed the gate to the horse pen with Lancelot still inside," Schmitz told the *Santa Clara Sentinel*. Although it was latched shut, it wasn't locked. "He figured out that if I don't lock the gate, he can ram it open if he butts it a few times. So that's what happened."

While Lancelot stuck around the ranch, Buddy and Harry took off for the great unknown. But Harry didn't have as much adventuresome spirit as Buddy. Harry was captured the next day after he got thirsty and wandered into a nearby meadow.

"Buddy's very elusive," said Schmitz at the time. "He's not like other horses. He's not attracted by meadows and other horses. He can stay hidden."

Boy, did he ever. No one could find him for days, giving Schmitz plenty of *whoa*. Friends and horse lovers from around the area went searching for Buddy from dawn to dusk. Calling his name, they trekked into ravines, rode horseback over the rugged landscape, and drove along nearby roads. Trying a new *tack*, Schmitz included Harry and Lancelot in the posse, hoping the scent of his animal friends would lure him into the open. If Buddy smelled anything, he figured it was fishy so he remained out of sight.

"One of the neighbors heard him snorting across the ravine one night," Schmitz said. "The next night someone saw him at Redwood Lodge. But by the time we would arrive, we would only find his tracks."

The big break came on day five. "Two members of the posse caught sight of him while riding by on horseback," she said. "He was hiding in some manzanita [evergreen shrubs] about a mile from the house," Schmitz said. Buddy's freedom run had ended, and he was captured without a hitch.

"When we got him back in the pen, he was particularly frisky, playful, and happy," Schmitz said. "I think he was glad to be back." Sure, because he now had a *stable* environment. As for Lancelot, hopefully he won't butt in again.

WELL-ROUNDED DOG

Dogs have been known to run around in circles, often chasing their tails. But Max the black Labrador retriever did something crazier. He *drove* around in circles. In reverse.

Max was riding shotgun while his owner was driving a Mercury Sable in Port St. Lucie, Florida, one afternoon in 2019. When they reached a cul-de-sac, the owner parked the car and, while leaving the engine running, got out to talk to someone.

Max wanted to get closer to the conversation, so he moved over to the driver's side and accidentally shifted the car into reverse. Because the front wheels were turned when the owner parked the vehicle, the Mercury began slowly circling the cul-de-sac backward.

The owner, who couldn't get into the car because the doors were locked, watched helplessly as Max sat in the front seat, seemingly enjoying the continuous, circular, backward ride—one that went on for nearly an hour.

The astonished owner called the police. When they arrived, there wasn't much they could do but suppress their laughter as the car did its merry-go-round.

"I figured, 'How the heck did he manage to do that?'" neighbor Anna Sabol told West Palm Beach TV station WPTV.

By now, several police cruisers had shown up. None of them had a backup plan. Meanwhile, Max was lapping up all the attention and enjoying his round-trip. "I laughed," Sabol said. "I thought they should give that dog a license to drive. He was a better driver than a lot of them I've seen."

Well, not exactly. Because the car was not making perfectly formed circles, it eventually inched its way toward the curb, knocking over a garbage can, mailbox, and a few decorative bricks. "He was doing pretty good until he hit the mailbox," said Sabol. "He went around for about an hour without hitting anything at all."

By striking the objects, the car had slowed enough so that an officer was able to run alongside it and enter a code on the keypad of the driver's side door. Opening the door, the officer slid inside, put the gear shift in park, and turned off the engine.

No one was hurt, said police, who posted on social media, "Max was fine, healthy, and happy!"

The dog certainly acted like he enjoyed it in a round-about way. "I saw the dog jump out of the car, wagging his tail," said Sabol. "I was like, 'Okay, good driving!'" Maybe so, but Max never learned to *parallel bark*.

PEN PALS

Some dogs miss their canine friends at doggy daycare so much they have played hooky from *home*. Yep, they ran away just so they could romp with their pals.

Hugo, a black Labrador retriever mix, was a regular boarder at Happy Tails Pet Hotel and Playland in St. Ann, Missouri. Although he loved his human family, he considered the daycare's other dogs and kindhearted staff a *wonder-fur* world.

One day in 2019 while Hugo was at home, he decided he wanted to spend time with his *pawesome* buds at Happy Tails, so he slipped away. He walked for several blocks and had to cross a busy thoroughfare to get to his destination.

On Facebook, the daycare posted, "Hugo ran away from home with only one thing on his mind . . . Happy Tails! Extremely lucky, Hugo ventured over a mile crossing a median on Lindbergh Blvd. to see all his friends. Hugo came sprinting onto our parking lot and into the front door following one of our employees! We are so glad Hugo wasn't hurt and told him next time to have his dad drive him! All dad could do was laugh as he picked Hugo up!"

Three years earlier, in Belmont, North Carolina, Riley, a five-year-old golden retriever, ran away from home and showed up unexpectedly at his favorite place— the Happy Dog Café Boutique & Spa.

Riley had been going to the daycare off and on for his whole life. "He's a sweet dog, and we love him," daycare owner Teresa McCarter told Charlotte TV station WBTV. And he loved playing with his fellow pooches.

One morning, while riding in the car with his owner, Tonia Mosteller, he grew excited when she neared the Happy Dog in downtown Belmont. Thinking she was going to drop him off there, he was greatly disappointed when they drove past it. "He kind of whimpered a little bit," Mosteller told WBTV. "He loves to play and he loves Happy Dog." When they returned home, "I gave him a treat while he was sitting on the back deck, and I said, 'Okay, buddy, I'll be back after a while.'" She left on an errand.

Not content to spend the afternoon home alone, Riley cleverly lifted the latch on the backyard gate and beelined it for more than a mile—including through much of downtown—straight to Happy Dog. The free-range rover knew the way because Mosteller often walked him there.

When he arrived, he sat down in front of the place. Recalled McCarter, "Someone walked in the door and said, 'There's a dog sitting outside waiting to come in.'" McCarter went over to see the dog and shouted, "Oh my gosh! It's Riley!" When she opened the door, Riley—his tail wagging wildly—bounded to the back room where he and his buddies had a ball.

"He just decided to put himself in daycare that day," she told WBTV. "His 'dad' said he'd come and get him, and I said, 'Oh, no. If Riley worked that hard to get here, then he's going to stay all day in daycare.'" And, no, it didn't cost his owners anything. Riley got away from home scot-free.

UDDERLY RIDICULOUS

If a runaway cow was going to hide out by a fast food restaurant, where would she go? Certainly not Burger King or McDonald's. No, she would head toward the eatery that any cow would deem the safest—Chick-fil-A.

A cow did just that in Noblesville, Indiana, in 2019 after breaking out of her transport trailer. And who could blame her for choosing Chick-fil-A? In its marketing campaigns, the fast food chain features cows urging customers to "Eat Mor Chikin" instead of consuming burgers.

When she escaped, the large white cow temporarily halted traffic in Noblesville where residents looked on in bemused surprise as officers chased after the runaway bovine.

Athena Hopkins and her husband, Michael, were among those in cars stuck in stalled traffic during the wild pursuit. She took out her phone and videoed this *mooving* experience.

In the video, which was posted on Facebook and went viral, the cow trots around in front of a city welcome sign before crossing a busy four-lane street that police had blocked off. Athena can be heard saying, "Who loses a cow in Noblesville?" Laughing, Michael replies, "I'm dying here." When the cow reaches the other side of the street, she heads straight for the Chick-fil-A, prompting Michael to ask, "Is this a promo for Chick-fil-A?"

No, it wasn't. But the cow sure milked it for all it was worth. She was soon captured and returned to her transport trailer. The cow definitely looked tired. After all, she was no spring chicken.

INTRUDERS

FAT CATS

Two cats in different countries repeatedly raided places that stored feline food. The sneaky eaters were so successful that they turned into heavyweights, which ultimately led to their captures and Internet notoriety.

Hercules wandered away from a house sitter in Portland, Oregon, in 2007 while his owner, Geoff Earnest, was out of town for two months. When Earnest returned home, there was no sign of the five-year-old silver tabby, leading the owner to believe the cat had died.

But Hercules was living large in more ways than one. For several months, he roamed during the day and then at night would slip through the doggy door of a garage in the suburb of Gresham and pig out on bags of food meant for six pet cats. At first the cats' owner, Jadwiga Drozdek, couldn't figure out why her felines were burning through the food.

"The food was disappearing very quickly," she told reporters. "I thought, 'Gosh, they're eating the same amount as always, so I don't understand why.'"

Hercules would *eat, drink, and be wary* in the garage while not being spotted. Ironically, it was his gluttony that caught up with him.

Drozdek first noticed Hercules in the garage at a moment when he couldn't escape—because he was tightly wedged in the doggy door. His head and shoulders were outside the door while his belly and tail were inside. This was a weighty problem. The cat had gained so many pounds that no matter how hard he tried he couldn't wriggle free.

"He was stuck!" Drozdek said. "Hilarious! And I was laughing!" She was also taking pictures of the flabby tabby. After she helped free him, she took him to the Oregon Humane Society because he had no identification. By now, he had tipped the scales at more than 20 pounds. He was so big that the shelter workers named him Goliath and invited the media to run stories about him, which created a Web sensation.

Back home in Portland, Earnest watched a TV newscast that featured a story about a rotund tomcat that got stuck in a doggy door. "I remember thinking, 'Wait a minute. That looks like Hercules. I thought he was dead,'" Earnest told the *Oregonian*. The following day, he was reunited with his long-lost pal. Although the shelter's veterinarian said Hercules needed to lose several pounds, Earnest claimed, "He's not fat. He's all muscle."

Besides, putting Hercules on a diet would be *wishful shrinking*.

Another runaway pet cat, this one named Clive, piled on the pounds after breaking into a pet food warehouse and binging for months on bags of kibble until his capture in 2016.

Clive, a nine-month-old Norwegian Forest kitten, disappeared from his home in Toton, Nottinghamshire, England, much to the heartache of his owners, Jonathan and Tanya Irons.

The couple put up posters around the neighborhood and asked Facebook followers to help find Clive. But no one had seen him. "We thought somebody must have taken him because he's such a lovely cat," Tanya told the *Daily Mirror*. "We lost hope of ever seeing him again."

After being gone for about a year, Clive sneaked into a warehouse, which was about two miles from the Irons's house. The cat probably thought he had died and gone to heaven. That's because, of all the buildings in the area, he had sneaked into the Kennelgate Pet Superstore warehouse, which contained more pet food than he could possibly consume in nine lifetimes.

For weeks, it was eat and run. He scarfed on boxes of cat edibles at night and scurried off to hide during the day in the huge 20,000-square-foot building. He kept to a diet of food made only for cats.

But his evening romps through the warehouse often triggered the burglar alarms. "We eventually found it was a cat that was setting off the alarms, but we just couldn't catch it," Colin Lewis, retail operations director, told the BBC. "We got a trap from a cat rescue center. It was a cage. We put some food in it, and then when the cat went in it, he stepped on a pressure pad that shut the cage door behind him."

Production supervisor Diane Gaskill told the *Daily Mirror*, "He was hissing and spitting, but he knew the game was up. We took him to the vet's where he was scanned for a microchip, and we were able to get the mobile number of his owner. I rang her straight away, and when I told her we found her cat, she couldn't believe it."

Clive had been missing for 14 months. When he was reunited with his owners, he had ballooned to nearly twice his original size, said Tanya. "I can't believe he's so porky. Clive was nine months old when we lost him, and he was a lot smaller then. We were shocked to see how big he had gotten. He's obviously been living the life of Riley in that pet food building."

Clive became reacquainted with his cat brothers George and Leon. "He wasn't a big eater before, but he always had to eat very quickly before his brothers stole the food," Tanya said. "At the warehouse, he was probably glad he didn't have to compete with them to eat for once.

"He has a huge appetite now. I've had to leave him with a big bucket of food because he just won't stop eating. We're not going to put him on a diet, though. Sure, he's a bit rounder. But he's happy." Yep, Clive's *feline good*.

PARTY ANIMALS

Bears have a habit of becoming uninvited guests, especially in hot tubs and pools.

A bruin helped himself to a dip in a Jacuzzi and a sip of an alcoholic drink while the homeowner looked on in disbelief.

Mark Hough was relaxing by his backyard hot tub in Altadena, California, and enjoying a freshly made margarita on a sunny afternoon in 2018. Boy, that looked mighty tempting to a bear that was peeking over a fence. Not bothering to wait for an invitation, the bear made his move.

"I got up, looked over in the bushes, and lo and

behold there's a bear climbing up over my fence," Hough told the *Pasadena Star-News*. Leaving behind his drink, Hough scurried into the house and watched as the bear lumbered into the Jacuzzi, which wasn't heated, although its jets were running.

For the next few minutes, the bear lounged in the tub, occasionally dunking his head in the water. "He was bobbing away in the Jacuzzi enjoying himself," Hough said. The bear played with the chlorinator and tossed the thermometer in the air while Hough recorded the intruder's antics. "He was having a grand old time."

Feeling thirsty, the bear emerged from the Jacuzzi and, after a brief tour of the backyard, helped himself to a cocktail. "He walked right over to the margarita, knocked it over, and lapped it up," Hough said.

But the bear wasn't ready to leave. After soaking in the tub and savoring a margarita, Pokey, as the bear was later named, was feeling a little drowsy, so he scaled a backyard tree and, as a *bear-faced lier*, took an hour-long nap. Afterward, the totally relaxed bear climbed down and ambled off into the woods.

The video was posted on Facebook and went viral. Among the comments: "Jacuzzi, steal a margarita, then go for a nap!!! Living the dream." "This bear is having a better summer than me." "This is just a modern-day Goldilocks story."

Obviously, the trespasser couldn't apologize for this intrusion. But if he could, he probably would have said, "Well, Jacuzzi me!"

The Basso family of Rockaway Township, New Jersey, had a wild backyard pool party. But they didn't throw it. No, a mama bear and her five cubs did.

The family's backyard featured a children's playground set and a large aboveground pool made of fabric and PVC pipe. It was meant for Tim, his wife, Justyna, and their two preschool daughters and friends. But one sweltering summer day in 2015 when the pool was unoccupied, the six black bears showed up unannounced. They climbed into the pool and played for about an hour.

"I thought they would drink out of it for a minute and then move on," Tim told Philadelphia TV station WPVI. "But they pretty much started climbing in. My first thought was, 'Where is the dog and where are the kids?'" Fortunately, they were all in the house where they watched helplessly as Justyna videoed the antics of the interlopers.

In the video, which went viral after it was posted on YouTube, the bears splash and wrestle in the water. Every so often, the cubs get out, climb over the playground set, skid down a plastic toy slide, and bat at the swing. Meanwhile, mama bear begins tossing inflatables and other items out of the pool. The cubs pounce on them, ripping and deflating them.

Three-year-old Sarah can be heard complaining, "Hey, they took my floaty."

Justyna, remaining calm, replies, "It's okay. They're just having fun." But later, when the mama juggles a device holding chlorine tabs and then wrangles with the hose, Justyna says, "Oh, that's not good."

"Bad, mommy bear, bad!" Sarah shouts.

"They're having the time of their life," Justyna says. "I'm not brave enough to tell them not to play with our stuff."

After about an hour, the mother bear left the yard with her little trespassers following her. "They came in, they experienced the pool, and they seemed to enjoy themselves," said Tim. "They did a little bit of damage on the pool toys and floats, but all in all I don't think it was a terrible experience." From the bears' point of view, the afternoon went swimmingly.

SWAN SONG

Most wild swans are content to paddle around in a pond or lake. But one male swan followed the beat of a different drummer. He waddled into an occupied vacation apartment, plopped down in the living room, and watched TV with its startled residents.

Dulcine Carney, an occupational therapist from Gorleston, Norfolk, England, was relaxing with her six-year-old niece, Sophie, in a villa in Sherwood Forest Center Parcs, an outdoor recreational area in Nottinghamshire, England, in 2019. Because it was a nice day, they left the sliding glass door open to the ground floor living room where Sophie was watching CBeebies, a British TV network geared toward young children, while Carney was napping on the sofa.

That's when Mr. Swan, who stood at least three feet high, came into the room and decided to join Sophie for a bird's-eye view of CBeebies. It's not every day that a little girl has a swan sit down beside her in the living room. Not sure what to do, she woke up her aunt.

"I was lying down on the couch with my eyes closed," Carney told the *Mansfield and Ashfield Chad* newspaper. "The next minute, Sophie whispered in my ear, 'Auntie, I need your help with the swan.' I thought she was having a joke, but when I opened my eyes, there was this swan standing next to her watching the telly.

"We weren't scared. We were very calm. I thought, 'Do I approach it?' It looked really calm but I did not want to upset it. It was really chill. It was just as if it was a puppy dog. It was about a meter [yard] away from me.

"Just then my [11-year-old] niece, Stephanie, came home, opened the door, and said, 'Why is there a swan in the villa?'"

That was a very good question, for which Carney had no immediate answer. Neither did she know the best way to get Mr. Swan to leave. He certainly wasn't in any hurry, especially since he was thoroughly enjoying CBeebies. After taking photos of the winged intruder, Carney grabbed a quilt and tried to use it as a shield as she gently urged him to return to his swan lake. "I went out of the villa and it followed me," she said. "It wasn't hissing or flapping. I just very gently patted it on its head and said goodbye." Mrs. Swan was waiting for him outside the villa.

Carney posted her photos on social media, and within hours they went viral.

In a classic understatement, a spokesperson from Center Parcs told the newspaper, "Our squirrels and swans tend to get quite comfortable around people." The feathered intruder didn't cause any more problems. His appearance in the villa was his swan song.

FACING THE MUSIC

A musically inclined bear broke into a home and played the piano.

Impawsible, you say? Well, it happened in 2017 after Katie Hawley of Vail, Colorado, left home and forgot to lock the kitchen window. That's a no-no because she lived in active bear country. When the bruin showed up, it easily opened the unlatched window and slipped inside.

As security camera video later revealed, the bear walked into the living room and spotted the upright piano. The intruder couldn't resist the urge to play. Rather than sit down on the bench, the bruin stood on its hind legs and banged on the keys. The music, if you could call it that, sounded nothing like ZZ Top's "Let Me Be Your Teddy Bear" or Jimi Hendrix's "Three Little Bears" or the theme song from the Paddington Bear movies.

As the *Washington Post* put it, "This was no Bear-thoven." At best, the intruder struck a chord, an ear-bending, one-note, awful chord.

Before the bear turned the living room into the animal's personal concert hall, it had opened the refrigerator and freezer drawer. It wolfed down a gallon bag of frozen strawberries and bananas, drank a bottle of maple syrup, snacked on a large package of chocolates, and even opened a jar of peanut butter and ate it. The trespasser eventually left through the open kitchen window.

When Hawley returned home and saw the mess, she assumed a burglar had broken into the residence, so she called police. The officer who was sent surveyed the scene and told her, "That was a bear, not a person." Security footage confirmed the identity of the intruder.

According to a Vail Police Department news release, "Following the report to police, the resident checked her internal camera system, which captured the event on video. The bear was seen wandering around the apartment and at one point went to a piano putting its paws on the keys, playing a few notes. The chords captured on video were unbearable, and the tune was equally grizzly."

And, besides, *his Bach was worse than his bite.*

NIGHT CRAWLER

A bear had a hankering for a midnight snack, so it opened an unlocked door of a house and raided the kitchen while two teenagers were watching television in a nearby room.

Hayes Sherman and his friend Bobby Harden, both 15, of San Francisco, were staying at a vacation cabin owned by Hayes's family in Truckee, California, in 2019. Even though a bear had ripped more than a dozen screens off the windows the previous year, the city boys had carelessly left the garage door open. The hungry bear took that as a welcome sign, entered the garage, and then opened the unlocked door that led to the kitchen.

The chewin' bruin lapped up all the berries that had been left in a bowl on the counter and then opened the refrigerator for some nighttime nibbles. A Nest camera in the living room videoed the black bear standing on its hind legs, sniffing around, and pawing through the refrigerator. The intruder broke open a Tupperware dish and gobbled up taco meat. Then it tore into pints of Ben & Jerry's ice cream—the Half Baked and Tonight Dough flavors—and polished off some crackers.

At first, the boys were unaware the marauding bear was in the next room until it began making too much noise. "I heard footsteps, and then I heard Tupperware being opened really loudly and aggressively," Hayes told Sacramento TV station KCRA. "The fridge started to beep because it was open too long." Looking through a sliding glass door that separated the TV room from the kitchen, the boys gasped in horror at seeing the bear.

"It looked us both in the eyes and it started coming toward us," Hayes said. "That was one of the scariest moments, coming face-to-face with the bear. I was really scared. I wasn't exactly sure what to do. I turned the TV off. We both went to the sliding door to hold it in place so that the bear couldn't get in."

The bear banged and scratched on the door several times while Hayes and Bobby struggled to hold it shut because it wouldn't lock. The teens didn't have their phones with them, so while they held on to the shaking door, Hayes used his Apple watch to call his mother, who was sleeping upstairs.

"I whispered to her, 'Mom, there is a bear in the house. Don't come downstairs,'" Hayes recalled. He hung up and called 911. "It was very difficult, because I was whispering to 911 on my watch in a very dark room while trying to hold the door closed so the bear couldn't get in," he said.

Thirteen minutes later, Placer County Sheriff's Deputy Allyson Prero arrived. She opened the unlocked front door, got out of the way, and let the bear exit the house. When the bear lingered in the driveway, Prero convinced the bruin to leave by firing a special shotgun shell that doesn't harm the animal but does cause some discomfort. The bear, who was hit in the backside, got the message.

"We came out, and we went to hug her, and we took a photo with her because we were just so grateful that she came to save us," Hayes said. Not pictured in the photo was what the bear left on the living room rug. That bear was a real stinker.

VEGGED OUT

A greedy groundhog who was videoed repeatedly sneaking into a man's garden and eating his vegetables was so brazen that, without a shadow of a doubt, he became an Internet sensation.

In the spring of 2019, veteran gardener Jeff Permar tended to his lush, fenced patch of veggies, herbs, and other produce behind his home in Middletown, Delaware, an example of *weed 'em and reap*. "It was a really good year in the garden," he told ABC News. "However, by the end of May, I started noticing the tops of the snap peas and other vegetables were chomped right off the top."

Permar had dealt with four-legged, veggie-loving villains before, but this one was different. It was eating a lot of produce and being wasteful, too. "I would have big giant tomatoes," he recalled in a YouTube video posted by thedodo.com. "He would take a chunk out of one and then move to the next one, take a chunk out, then go on to the next one."

Not finding tracks that could help identify the culprit, Permar set up a ground-level video camera that would record whenever it detected any movement. The next day, he received a notification on his phone from the camera. It had identified the intruder. The culprit was munching on a cucumber.

"I look, and it's this groundhog," Permar said. "He pops right up out of nowhere and starts eating. Smacks his lips and stares into the camera. He's like, 'I'm eatin' your garden. What are you gonna do about it?' At first, I was really upset. I put the fence higher. I put logs around the fence to prevent animals from coming in underneath it. And he was still getting in. He was coming by at least three times a day. He always parked in the same spot and always stared into the camera."

By eating Permar's produce right in front of the camera, it was as if the groundhog was taunting him. But every day, when Permar looked at new video, he became less upset. "I actually started to look forward to seeing him," the gardener said. "It took only about a week or so for him to win my heart over. I was like, 'This guy is awesome. He can have whatever he wants.'"

The trespasser had dug himself a comfy hole underneath the nearby garden shack and made it his home. Then he launched his daily raids on the garden.

Because the groundhog liked to take chunks out of tomatoes, Permar decided to call him a corny name—Chunk. "This guy is so cute, how could you get mad at him?" he told ABC.

The gardener decided if you can't *beet* him, join him. The groundhog almost always ate in front of the camera, so Permar figured animal lovers would enjoy seeing Chunk up close and personal. He posted videos on a YouTube channel devoted solely to the produce pilferer, and viewers began rooting for him.

"People fell in love with him," Permar said. "They

were looking forward to starting their day by watching Chunk eat. I was getting comments like 'This really brightened my day.' The videos reached all around the world.

"Chunk plops himself right in front of the camera every time and devours our produce," Permar said on social media. "The messier the food, the better. He's so sloppy and loud, and chomping and smacking. If a human was eating like that, I would have to leave the room. But if Chunk's doing it, it's kind of cool. Chunk don't care and Chunk don't eat junk. He doesn't mess with the herbs and he doesn't touch the peppers at all. Tomatoes and carrots are his absolute favorite."

The gardener wondered who would *turnip* next. Later that summer, Permar noticed something new on the video feed. Chunk was eating in front of the camera with a companion. "I said, 'What?'" Permar recalled. "They're hugging and kissing and fighting and talking back like in a real relationship." Permar named the female groundhog Nibbles.

"It's like he told Nibbles, 'Hey, I've got a spot where we can fatten up for the winter. Come on over.'" In November, the happy couple snuggled into the hole that Chunk had made to ride out the cold weather.

Over the winter, Permar reinforced the garden to keep critters out for the spring of 2020. However, he created a separate garden for Chunk, Nibbles, and their family so they could enjoy *peas and quiet*. "They can do whatever," Permar said. "We can coexist. This is their land, too." The gardener and the groundhogs *romaine* friends.

SWEET SPOTS

A bear with a hankering for sweets couldn't wait for Christmas, so it raided a freezer and devoured holiday treats that a woman had been making and storing for days.

Professional baker Sharla Marr of Campbell River, British Columbia, Canada, loved the holidays because this was the time when she would bake all sorts of special goodies to give to family and friends as gifts and to sell to customers.

Beginning in early December 2019, Marr began making her sugary creations and storing them in her freezer, which was located outside in her carport. She had planned to distribute and sell the baked goods closer to Christmas.

But a bear decided there was *no crime like the present*. About a week after Marr had started making her Christmas creations, the bear showed up late at night, opened the freezer, and helped itself to a belly full of holiday delights.

The freezer also contained salmon, other fish, and

blackberries. Normally those foods would make the perfect bear meal. But this intruder had such a sweet tooth that all it cared about were the Christmas treats. It ate more than two pounds of peanut brittle, a large pan of Canadian chocolate treats known as Nanaimo bars, and a big batch of chocolate truffles.

"The bear had eaten about half of my Christmas baking," Marr told CTV News. "It also ate some meat and bread products." That cost her a lot of dough.

When the bear finished its festive feast, it walked off without having the decency to close the freezer door, ruining most everything inside. As a thank-you, the trespasser left a smelly present.

"That was the cherry on top of everything—the fact that it had not only eaten everything but also had pooped on my doorstep," Marr said. "It was quite rude."

Marr, who said she had no idea bears could open doors, put a lock on the freezer.

She had a message for the bear: "I hope it was good. I hope you enjoyed it. I hope you get sick." Marr finally got over her anger when she figured it was *mind over batter*.

There's a famous line in the movie *Forrest Gump* that goes, "Life is like a box of chocolates. You never know what you're gonna get."

Four bears loved what they got.

Lilly Thurmond, 16, of Asheville, North Carolina, had left a box containing fifty chocolate bars in her unlocked Prius, which was parked in the driveway of her home. Lilly, a high school junior, had planned to sell the individually wrapped bars to help raise money for the upcoming prom.

While relaxing in her home one Sunday afternoon in 2018, she looked out the window and saw a mama bear and her cubs. Living in a wooded area in western North Carolina, Lilly was used to seeing the bruins. What she wasn't used to seeing were bears breaking into a vehicle—especially hers. She caught them with *their paws in the candy car.*

After the bears opened the right rear door and entered the Prius, Lilly whipped out her cell phone and began recording the intrusion from an upstairs window. There was little else she could do other than scream in frustration, which she did.

In the video, which she shared with local TV station WLOS, she cries out in a high-pitched voice, "I don't even understand why there are bears in my car! There're three bears in my car at the moment. Three! Oh, there comes another one!"

One of the bears opened the front door and got in. The door closed behind it. Inside, the mama and her brood ripped open the wrappings and devoured the candy bars one by one. The intruders savored all three flavors—almond, milk chocolate, and dark chocolate. Then they exited the car and disappeared into the woods, leaving one lone candy bar for Lilly.

When she went out to inspect her car, she saw that the interior was filthy and had dozens of punctures from bear claws. Fortunately, insurance covered the damage.

As for the burglars, by not eating the candy bars all at once, they didn't *choke a lot*.

VILLAINS

A RAVEN MANIAC

Izabella, or Izzie for short, has been one of England's most notorious winged criminals. Over the years, the raven from Knaresborough Castle, North Yorkshire, boasts a rap sheet that includes such crimes as stealing cell phones, babies' pacifiers, and golf balls; terrorizing and swearing at visitors; and swiping and eating people's food. She even took a photo from a camera that she stole.

"What can I say about Izzie," said Igraine Hustwitt Skelton, Her Majesty's Keeper of Castle Ravens. "She is the raven world's answer to a hyperactive child."

The dozen ravens that were cared for at the castle were often allowed to sit outside without being tethered because they were so well behaved and posed no problem to visitors. But all that changed thanks to Izabella. "Due to the continued disruptive behavior by this particular young lady, the ravens now have to be fastened when on public display," Skelton said on the castle's website, knaresboroughcastleravens.webs.com.

"It all started off lighthearted," Skelton continued. "Izzie greeted people in her own special way by flying onto people's shoulders and saying hello to them. But after a while, she stopped doing this and instead would launch herself at any visitor who stopped to look at her." In other words, Izzie caused a huge flap by dive-bombing visitors, forcing them to duck or scurry out of her way.

She seemed to have a devilish delight in making children cry. She'd swoop down and snatch pacifiers from baby carriages. One of her favorite places to provoke tears was at the castle's pitch and putt, a scaled-down golf course. "She left many children crying because she had taken their golf balls," said Skelton. "She would fly down to the river, drop them in the water, then fly back for another one. I had to have a pocket full of golf balls to replace the ones Izzie flew off with."

She ruffled the feathers of the castle's lawn bowlers, too, by getting in their way or trying to distract them just as they were ready to roll their ball. "I spent most of my time shooing her off the bowling green so people could play uninterrupted," Skelton said.

Izzie could crow that she was an impish con artist. "One Saturday, I was busy chatting with a local resident when Izzie decided to get into some mischief," recalled her handler. "She spotted a potential victim, and, like a spider drawing a fly into its web, Izzie did likewise with this poor unsuspecting visitor."

The rascally raven flew to a trash can, pulled out an empty plastic bottle, and brought it to her favorite spot on the bowling green. Once there, she stuck her foot in the bottle, lay on the ground, and started to caw. "This lady was on a seat overlooking the bowling green, eating her fish and chips when she saw Izzie was in some distress—or so she thought," Skelton recounted. "Rushing to her aid, the woman had left her lunch and camera on the seat."

As the woman neared Izzie, the bird kicked off the bottle and zoomed to the vacated seat. Surprisingly, the raven ignored the fish and chips and instead focused on the big prize—the woman's camera. With the camera in her powerful beak, Izzie flew to the museum roof where she perched with her stolen property. "By this time, I was aware of what was going on and rushed to the lady, apologizing for the naughty raven," said

Skelton. "It was some twenty minutes before Izzie let go of the camera, and it slid down the roof and into our waiting hands." And, yes, the raven had taken a photograph using her beak.

Izzie took on the role of *Lord of the Wings*. In a 2015 interview, Skelton joked, "Izzie has quite a reputation in Knaresborough as being the only bird in the locality to get an ASBO [anti-social behavior order issued by the court].

"It is a shame that she started to fly at people because she had many visitors in stitches with her playfulness. She would walk along the wall of the bowling green with a stone in her foot, dragging it as if to say her [leash] was her ball and chain. She would fly down to the river near the Marigold Cafe and terrorize the ducks. She pinched [stole] sandwiches from people who dared to picnic opposite her perch. She is eight now and shows no sign that she might grow out of it."

Because ravens are considered among the smartest birds in the world, they can mimic sounds and human speech. "She would fly around the castle grounds, asking people below, 'What's the matter?'" Skelton said. "Alas, she is now using [foul language] in her speech, which is not appropriate with so many young children around."

Izzy learned to swear from listening to visitors, said her keeper. "Now when people try to take her picture, she'll say what the [swear word] are you looking at, [swear word]. One time, she flew to the police station nearby and perched outside and said really loud, 'Ello, ello, ello!' When the constable came out to take a look, she swore at him."

She even has frustrated the castle gardeners by pulling up young flowers that had just been planted.

Despite her troubling tomfoolery, Izzie has a legion of admirers. "She's got her own fan club of people who come to see her every year and followers from America and Canada," said Skelton. "Izzie even has her own Facebook page."

But as she grew older, Izzie seemed to mature. If she could speak about committing similar crimes like those from her past, quoth the raven, "Nevermore."

OH, DEER ME!

A deer making a mad dash through a parking lot slammed into an unsuspecting man, flattening him before making a clean getaway.

"It was absolutely nuts," mugging victim Ken Worthy told WSOC, a TV station in Charlotte, North Carolina.

On a sunny winter day in 2020, Worthy and his wife, Dee, of Locust, North Carolina, were walking toward their car, each carrying a cup filled with a soft drink from McDonald's. They were unaware that an antlered troublemaker was heading their way.

Moments earlier, the deer had plowed into the front door of the Dandy Walrus Electric Tattoo shop. Surprisingly, the door didn't break, although the impact startled the customers inside. "It hit so hard that it shook the shop," owner Jason Smith told the *Charlotte Observer*. "There was so much deer fur flying around that it looked like smoke."

But the buck didn't stop there. He dashed off and rammed the door of a nearby medical rehab business so hard that he lost an antler. Sprinting across the parking lot toward the woods, the deer had no intention of veering off course—never mind that an innocent man was already in the animal's path.

Worthy, a retired police detective, looked both ways as he and his wife approached their car. He didn't see the deer hightailing it toward him until it was too late. To his credit, the buck tried his best to jump over Worthy. But the animal badly misjudged his leaping abilities. Going airborne way too soon, the deer was on his downward arc when he crashed into Worthy, knocking him flat to the pavement.

"It was just a bit of brown, and then I saw his face," Worthy told WSOC. "I was down on the ground. It happened that quick. I mean, you can just see the flash of him rolling over me and in a straight line, and he was gone," Worthy said.

When they collided, the deer did a face-plant but then scrambled to his feet and took off in a hit-and-run that was caught on McDonald's security cameras. In the video, which Worthy shared on Facebook, the deer lays the man out on his rear end, but Worthy rolls over and bounces up on his feet, all the while never letting go of his covered soft drink. His wife, who was walking only a few feet behind him, rushes over to see if he is all right.

"Life is crazy sometimes," Worthy said on Facebook. "Not injured. PS—Didn't spill my Coke!" As he explained on TV, "There are important things in your life, and Diet Coke is one of them."

It's a memory that will always remain *deer to his heart.*

FREE LUNCH

Two dogs were hungry, so when they saw an unattended postal truck, they addressed the situation by jumping into the vehicle and eating the mail carrier's lunch.

Bear and Bull, black Labrador-mastiff mixes, made it a habit of trying to get into delivery and postal trucks that stopped at the rural home of their owner, Carol Jordan, in Smithfield, Virginia. The dogs were always hounding the drivers, begging them for a treat or two because, to them, anything edible was dog food. Even when their bellies were full, they were on the prowl for a free lunch.

One day in 2018, Jordan was running errands while the dogs were relaxing in the front yard of the electronically-fenced-in five-acre spread. Just then, a mail carrier named Mary drove up and parked her postal truck by the house. Bear and Bull watched Mary leave the vehicle to place a package by the front door. Seizing the opportunity, the dogs leaped into the truck in search of food. Within seconds, they had scored Mary's lunch. By the time she returned to her vehicle, her meal had been devoured.

Rather than go postal, Mary was concerned about the dogs' welfare because her lunch wasn't really canine food. So on a delivery slip, she wrote a note to Jordan explaining what the dogs had done and put it by the package.

The note read, "Hey! I drove up to deliver a package and both of the dogs crawled in my truck. They got into my lunch and ate an egg and some carrots and pumpkin seeds. I don't know if that will upset their tummies, just FYI!"

When Jordan came home, the dogs—she refers to

them as "the boys"—appeared shamefaced. But that was nothing new. "The boys always look guilty, so we would never have known anything went on if Mary hadn't left the note," Jordan told InsideEdition.com.

"When we first saw the note, our initial thought was, 'What did they do now?' They try to get into everyone's car that comes up our driveway. They have climbed into the FedEx truck and sat in the driver's seat and passenger seat like they were going on a joyride." But only after first searching for food, of course.

Jordan went on social media to shame the boys. Then she wrote a note of her own, attached it to a $20 Subway gift card, and left it at the post office because at the time she didn't know the identity of the mail carrier. The note said, "Sorry we ate your lunch. Thank you for sharing! Bull & Bear Jordan. P.S. Our humans said thank you for leaving a note. We didn't like the note. We got in trouble." The note ended with a sad face.

"We felt bad that they ate her lunch," Jordan said. "We wanted to make it up to her. We live in the country, and everyone here is friendly and looks out for each other. It was the right thing to do."

Ever since the family rescued Bull and Bear six years earlier from a high-kill shelter, the two were always getting into mischief. "They have chased mice and lizards into three riding lawn mowers and totally gutted the lawn mowers," Jordan said. "They pulled all of our downspouts off our house as puppies. They constantly dig craters in our yard when going after moles and much more." She said Bull, the smaller of the two brothers, took on the role of ringleader of the troublemakers.

They have been such characters that Jordan set up a Bear and Bull Jordan Facebook page, posting photos of their antics. "So many people have commented that it brightened their day or that the boys remind them of dogs they had but are now passed on," she said. "We are floored by the amount of attention it has received."

As the saying goes, every dog has its day.

NUT CASE

If Burton the squirrel could talk, he would have said something like: "I'm gonna make you an offer you can't refuse. Let me and three of my buddies protect your place of business for a small price—all the nuts we want. You wouldn't want somethin' bad to happen to your establishment, now would ya?"

Have A Banana Trading Company, a fresh fruit and vegetable stand in Manchester, England, was having a problem in 2019 with a few brazen squirrels. They were raiding its outdoor nut display case, which contained cubbyholes with plastic flaps for different kinds of nuts, dried berries, and trail mix. The squirrels were jumping up onto the display and running off with various snacks. That wasn't good for business. After all, what customer wants to select nuts from nooks that had been raided by wild squirrels. Besides, nuts aren't cheap. Some of them can cost *an almond a leg*.

The owner tried to shoo away the squirrels, but these nutjobs were persistent and kept returning to snare the goodies. It was as if they were criminals saying, "Give me all the cashews you've got." Eventually the owner realized his efforts were futile. The only way to save the nuts in the display case and to keep his paying customers happy was to "negotiate" with the head squirrel—a large bushy rodent that he called Burton.

The owner made a pact with the head squirrel. The fruit and vegetable stand would dedicate one cubbyhole solely for Burton and his gang—no humans—in exchange for leaving the rest of the nut nooks alone for regular customers. The squirrels would be free to get as many nuts as they wanted from their own little compartment.

To his Instagram followers, the unnamed owner posted photos of Burton with the caption, "If you can't beat them . . ." The post added, "This is one of four squirrels that visit. By some freak coincidence, all are called Burton, or at least that's what I think they said."

Another photo showed that on the outdoor display

case, signs on each flap covering the nooks named the kinds of food items they contained. A cubbyhole on the bottom row of the display case between the Bombay mix and the sriracha peas was labeled "Burton the Squirrel." Ignoring the bagged peanuts in the other compartments, Burton, Burton, Burton, and Burton have been videoed opening the flap to their cubbyhole, grabbing loose nuts, and leaving.

In a nutshell, the arrangement is indeed all that it was cracked up to be.

CROW'S FEAT

Edgar the bird had something to crow about—mugging people and getting away with it.

The bandit was a wily wild crow who hung out at a Wawa convenience store in Cherry Hill, New Jersey, in 2019. Perched above the entrance, he would swoop down and act friendly toward his unsuspecting mark. Then, in a flash, he would snatch whatever they had in their hands and fly off with it.

One day, Philadelphia musician Curtis Remarc pulled up to the store and noticed that a man was pointing up at the Wawa sign. A crow was sitting in one of the Ws, holding a rolled-up dollar bill in his beak and looking down on the man, who kept shouting, "Drop it!

Drop it!" Judging by the way the bird seemed to enjoy the situation, it was as if the feathered fiend considered the buck funny money.

Getting out his cell phone, Remarc began videoing the scene of the crime and walked over to the victim, who said, "I can't believe Edgar stole from me."

"The bird's name is Edgar?" Remarc asked.

"Yes," replied the man. "I call him that. I was feeding him yesterday, and now he took my dollar." And the bird had no intention of giving it back. The victim finally gave up and left.

"It seems Edgar is on a bit of a crime streak," reported phillyvoice.com at the time. "This morning he stole someone's cigarette, too, and keeps sticking [stolen items] in the V part of the Ws. Edgar the Crow seems like the kind of bird Philadelphia can get behind as a convenience store mascot. He's got plenty of sass . . . and now he has a dollar."

According to thedodo.com, a store manager told Remarc that Edgar often mugged customers in the Wawa parking lot and stashed the loot in the Wawa sign. "The thefts don't always go as planned, though," the manager said. "Just the day before this dollar heist, Edgar had gotten his beak stuck in someone's car window."

On his morning show on WPG Radio, personality Dave Van Camp warned customers about the flighty bird. "Who knows what else Edgar could have stashed away? Lottery tickets? Hats? Maybe a toupee? And who knows if he also likes poaching items from customers walking in and out of the McDonald's, which is located next door. As of now, there doesn't seem to be a warrant out for Edgar's arrest, but if you visit the Wawa on Route 38 in Cherry Hill, hold on to your cash and any other valuables that a crow may want to get his beak on."

Luckily for Edgar, he didn't become a jailbird.

COP OUT

A four-legged escapee who had been collared by a police officer did not want to go to jail—so he commandeered the cop car.

A pit bull had sneaked out of his owner's home and was running throughout the neighborhood when the Kilgore (Texas) Police Department received a call that a possible dangerous animal was on the loose. A man had called police the previous week about a pit bull that had jumped into his car and "hijacked" it. In that case, the dog finally gave up and was returned home.

During the latest call, a police officer was dispatched to capture the canine delinquent. Not knowing the name of the dog, the police department referred to him as Cujo, named after the Stephen King novel and movie about a killer dog that goes on a rampage.

What happened next in Kilgore made news throughout the region. Here's the way police chief Todd Hunter described the 2019 incident on Facebook: "The Officer located this dog running at large and thought he might be able to quickly capture it. He opened his back door and tried to coax the critter into the back seat, which is caged.

"In his haste, the Officer also left the driver's door open. Cujo decided he wasn't going to jail and instead jumped into the front seat. As the Officer tried to get him out of the front driver's seat, Cujo became aggressive. The door was shut to prevent injury to the dog or Officer.

"The Officer's car had been hijacked!!! This critter wasn't coming out . . . He was now enjoying the A/C and the Officer's beef jerky.

"After hearing some strange radio traffic about this hijacking, I asked some questions over the radio. Moments later, the Officer texted me a picture of the situation . . . I texted back that the dog didn't look happy. The Officer texted with this statement, 'He ain't, and neither am I.' Good news is that the Animal Control Officer arrived and safely took Cujo into custody. The only injury sustained in this incident was to the Officer's pride. LOL."

The dog was brought to an animal shelter while officers tried to find his owner. They joked that bail would be a new package of beef jerky to replace the one that he scarfed down.

Two days later, the police department posted this Facebook message: "Today the Pit Bull that hijacked one of our Police cars has been reunited with his Dad. After our brief encounter, we named him Cujo. We learned from the animal shelter he was really a loving critter. He was most probably scared after escaping his yard. His real name is Chato, and he is home resting after being bailed out. According to Google, Chato means a boring or an annoying person. Chato was anything but boring Saturday night. We are so glad he has been reunited with his Dad."

For Chato, his *ruff day* was over, and all was *fur-given*.

DON'T BET ON IT

A racehorse bolted from her rider and burst into, of all things, a sports betting bar.

The young unnamed filly was being trained at the world-famous Chateau de Chantilly near Paris in 2018 where she gained a reputation for running away. Her trainer, Jean-Marie Beguigne, told the newspaper

Ouest-France that a rider was directing her from a stable toward the Chantilly Racecourse, which she had never run on before. But something spooked her, so she reared up, causing her rider to fall to the ground.

With no one in the saddle, the chestnut horse galloped off in a one-horse race. She ran along a busy road, crossed a roundabout, and went down a street (no, not *Mane* Street). Turning a corner, she headed for the bar, which was about a half mile from the stables.

Looking out the window, customers and staff at first laughed at the riderless steed. They never imagined that she would charge through the front door. But that's exactly what she did. "She came in by pushing open the door," Stéphane Jasmin, owner of the business, told the newspaper.

With her saddle slipping off, the dark horse kicked her back legs and stormed through the bar, prompting the five customers at tables to scramble for the safety of the other side of the lengthy counter where three employees were seeking refuge. As tables and chairs crashed to the floor, she galloped to a spot in the far corner of the bar at a spot where minutes earlier more than a dozen customers had placed their bets on computerized machines for upcoming horse races. Whether she would have bet on herself if she had the money, no one will ever know.

"Then the filly turned around, breaking a table

and chairs," Jasmin recalled. Still kicking her back legs, she dashed out the open door and ended up at a parking lot where she settled down. Fortunately, neither she nor the customers were hurt. After she was easily captured, the filly was walked back to what is known as the Great Stables (where, by the way, several scenes were shot for the 1985 James Bond movie *A View to a Kill*.)

But what happened in the betting bar was more bizarre and unbelievable than anything in the movie. Said Jasmin, "This is the first time that this story has happened in the world!"

BONEHEADS

TRASH TALK

A bear that townspeople nicknamed T-Shirt was down in the dumps literally and needed help from the police.

The huge black bear, who got his name because of the white fur on his chest, had a reputation for spending his nights out on the town in Kings Beach, California. That meant he went dumpster diving often. He knew how to open the lids of metal trash bins and scavenge for scraps. But one night in 2019, while the bruin was enjoying the garbage in a dumpster, the lid fell, snagged on a chain, and locked him in.

He tried to get out, but all he could do was open a hatch on the lid, allowing him to stick his big head out. But that's as far as he could get. Unable to escape, T-Shirt began wailing in a *bearitone* voice, waking up residents in a nearby apartment building at 3 a.m. Because nobody wanted to mess with a 400-pound black bear, a concerned citizen called Placer County deputies.

When the officers arrived, they turned on a video recorder to document their attempt to rescue the bear. The video, which the Placer County Sheriff's Office posted on Facebook, shows Deputy Joe Bertoni cautiously approaching the dumpster when it suddenly begins shaking. Then the bear pops his head out of the hatch, causing the deputy to shout, "Whoa!" as he scampers back out of camera range.

The bear ducks under the hatch and then pops up again. "That's T-Shirt," says Bertoni. "He has a big white front on him." The deputies knew all about T-shirt. He had several run-ins with the law in the small town, which is located on the banks of Lake Tahoe. Usually he would try to raid dumpster. Yep, he'd *bin there and dumped* that.

Bertoni and his partner, Deputy Dan Staley, needed to unhook the chained latch to the double lid. But they didn't want to get too close to the bin. When T-shirt ducked down into the dumpster, Bertoni grabbed a long tree branch and, from as far away as possible, used it like a pole, trying to unchain the latch.

The video shows that as Bertoni works on the latch, Staley, who is on the other side of the dumpster, says, "Dude, I am so going to run (once the bear is freed)."

Bertoni finally gets the latch unchained. But T-Shirt still can't get out until both lids are open. While Staley momentarily distracts the bear, Bertoni goes to the other side of the dumpster, carefully flips open the lid, and sprints out of camera view. "There we go," says Staley. "Nice, Joe."

T-Shirt looks around but doesn't try to escape right away. "He'll figure it out," says Bertoni.

"Not if he goes back in," Staley replies.

Finally, T-Shirt manages to free himself and tumble out of the dumpster. "There we go," says one of the deputies. "There he goes. Come on, attaboy. Good boooy!"

The bruin, known to have a rather growly attitude, was hardly grateful. He glowered at the deputies and even took a couple of swipes at them, Sheriff's Sergeant Dave Hunt told the *Los Angeles Times*. "A little too close for my taste," he said. "He's not a friendly bear by any means. I think he was just tired."

Hunt said T-Shirt had gained weight, which was understandable because it was near the time when bears go into hibernation. "He's a pretty big boy," said Hunt. "How he got in is beyond me. If he was a little bit skinnier, he could have gotten out."

No doubt the ordeal made T-shirt feel like trash.

HIGH HORSE

Holly the horse had a hankering for a midnight snack, so she trotted up the stairs to the hayloft and helped herself to a pile of hay. But she learned that what goes up doesn't necessarily come down—at least not very easily.

Because horses have poor depth perception, she couldn't use the stairs to go back down. She was stuck in the hayloft. The only way to get her down required a complicated four-hour rescue effort involving heavy equipment.

Holly, a 12-year-old beige Welsh Percheron cross, lived on a farm near Luray, Virginia. She seldom got into any trouble unless it involved food. Although she was well fed, she had an unbridled appetite.

One evening in 2018, Holly discovered that one of the other horses had pushed a barricade aside and cracked open a barn door. When that horse left, Holly realized the door was ajar wide enough for her to squeeze through. Once inside, she couldn't rein in her desire to eat, so she headed for the loft where the hay was stored.

The horse clomped up the relatively narrow wooden steps, worked her way through the tight turn of a small landing, and reached the loft. Then she helped herself to all the hay she wanted until she was stuffed. (A bad case of hay fever?)

Holly was a smart horse and knew she'd get in trouble for gobbling up the hay in the loft. She also had enough horse sense not to return down the steps because she wasn't trained to descend a stairway. There was an opening in the loft that led to a wooden balcony, but she wasn't about to go out there and jump more than 20 feet to the ground. No, she was stuck and would have to wait until morning for help.

When the owner, who asked to remain anonymous, heard from the horse's mouth that Holly was in the loft, the woman went online. She found the answer to getting the high horse down—the Little Fork Volunteer Fire & Rescue's Large Animal Rescue Team, the only volunteer squad of its kind in the entire state. Its members were only an hour away.

Headed by Fire Chief Doug Monaco, the four-person team arrived, along with a local veterinarian and members of the Luray Volunteer Fire Department and the Page County Sheriff's Office. "It's such an oddity, it really is, to have a horse in a hayloft," Monaco told the *Fredericksburg Free Lance-Star.*

Two years earlier, the team faced a similar situation when a horse was stuck upstairs in a barn in Botetourt County. In that case, they sedated the horse and slid it on a blanket down a wide set of steps.

But Holly's case was different because the steps were so narrow with walls on each side of them. The rescue squad looked at their options. They could rig a pulley system and lower Holly down the stairs. "If we used this, Holly would have to be heavily sedated for both her and our safety," Monaco said. "There was also a risk of her becoming trapped in the 90-degree turn about six feet from the bottom.

"Plan B was to remove the wall and build a ramp using three-quarter-inch plywood to slide Holly safely to the ground." But that would have taken hours to do.

Fortunately, the owner's neighbor, Garrett Moyer, offered to bring over his telehandler, sort of a cross between a forklift and a cherry picker with a telescopic boom often used to put hay in the loft. "This machine was large enough, could extend 30 feet and lift 4,400 pounds," Monaco said. "This became Plan C."

Holly tried to remain calm with all these strangers showing up. "Every once in a while, she would make horse noises because she missed her buddies," he said.

While Moyer drove the telehandler to the scene, rescuers removed the balcony railing. Then the veterinarian injected Holly with a sedative to help keep her relaxed. After bringing her out to the balcony, they fitted her with lifting straps and a head protector. The straps were attached to a bar on the boom. Holly was lifted about four feet off the balcony and then lowered to the ground. "Holly seemed apprehensive when she was moved off the balcony and found herself twenty feet off the ground, but she remained calm," Monaco said.

Once Holly was back on firm soil, the rescuers removed the slings. The horse walked off and wanted nothing more than a long nap.

The next day, Moyer posted on Facebook, "I've unloaded a lot of things with this machine, but this was my first horse."

As for Holly, it was a *night mare*.

ALL WASHED UP

Felix the cat went into serious tailspins when he jumped in a washing machine and was tossed around for an entire wash cycle. If it's true that cats have nine lives, he was down to eight after his ordeal unfolded.

The one-year-old Hemingway cat (a feline with six toes on each paw) was one of three cats owned by Stefani Carroll-Kirchoff of Maplewood, Minnesota. "He's lovable, but he does get himself into trouble," she said.

Felix often followed her to the basement when she did the laundry. Normally, she checked the machine to make sure no cat had slipped inside before she turned it on. But one day in 2019 while tossing 10 items of dirty laundry in the wash, she turned her back for only a few seconds. That's all it took for Felix to hop into the machine without being noticed.

Unaware that her black-and-white cat had snuggled on the soiled clothes and towels for a little nap, Carroll-Kirchoff closed the lid and set the dial to express wash to save some time and water. For the next 45 terrifying minutes, poor Felix was tossed around, flipped, and battered in soapy water.

When his owner returned and opened the lid, she screamed in horror at seeing her soaked, nearly dead cat wrapped around a twisted towel. Battered and bruised, Felix could hardly breathe because his lungs were waterlogged, and he could barely see because his eyes were clouded with chemical burns from the detergent.

"I'm still traumatized," Carroll-Kirchoff told the *Star-Tribune* days after the emotionally draining incident.

She was amazed that Felix was still alive, knowing that had she put the machine on the longer regular wash, which also uses more water, the cat likely would have died.

Felix was rushed to the Animal Emergency and Referral Center of Minnesota in Oakdale where he was placed in an oxygen chamber and given an IV as well as medicine for his damaged eyes. The vets feared he would get pneumonia and be permanently blind. But Felix had a strong will to live. Thanks to an online GoFundMe appeal, the family was able to pay for the $1,000-a-day medical expenses.

After eight days in the animal hospital, Felix was healthy enough to return home.

"He's doing phenomenally," Carroll-Kirchoff told the newspaper six weeks later. "He's a normal cat, still into mischief. He still greets us at the door every day like always."

She said his lungs had healed, and although his eyes were cloudy from corneal damage, he was able to see well enough to jump around and play with toys. Just last week she found him balancing on top of an open door. "He's as feisty as ever."

Carroll-Kirchoff said she hoped Felix's misfortune will alert pet owners to the dangers of leaving washers and dryers unattended. She also donated money left over from the online fundraiser to charities that assist families with pet emergencies. "There's no way I can repay what's been done for Felix," she said. "I'm just so grateful to everyone. I can't believe there are that many good people in this world. Felix wouldn't be alive without the support and prayers and good wishes of everyone out there."

The owner made the laundry room off-limits to the cats because she didn't want them to get into a load of trouble.

A month later, another feline, Comet, a five-month-old kitten who lived with Perry and Naomi Thompson of Gillingham, Kent, England, got lost in the wash. Looking for a new place to spend a good night's sleep, the cat noticed the door to the front-loading washing machine was open, so he jumped inside and dozed off among the dirty clothes. Early the next morning, Naomi shut the door and turned on the washing machine.

Soon she heard terrible noises and realized they were frenzied muffled meows. After a frantic search, she discovered the distressing cries were coming from Comet inside the washing machine. Naomi unleashed a bloodcurdling scream, waking up Perry, who rushed to her side, fearing someone was trying to break into the house.

"Naomi was horrified," Perry told KentOnline. "The washing machine door was locked, but she found the strength to rip it off. She said Comet was in the washing machine, but I couldn't see anything. I put my hand into the water and felt his tail among the clothes right at the bottom of the big drum.

"He wasn't breathing, and his eyes were wide open. I

honestly thought he was gone. Just at that moment, though, he twitched. I put him on the kitchen floor and started doing CPR. It was the only thing I could think of to try to bring him back to life. I was pumping his chest and breathing into his mouth, and, thankfully, he came 'round."

Perry brought Comet to emergency animal clinic Vets Now in Gillingham. "Comet was in a pretty bad way when he came in," veterinarian nurse Victoria Camburn told KentOnline.

"He was disoriented and wheezing, so we put him straight into an oxygen tent and gave him fluid therapy. We were concerned about pneumonia, but thankfully the ultrasound scan showed there was no fluid in the lungs or in his abdomen. The other diagnostic tests, however, showed issues with his breathing and an electrolyte imbalance, which we treated."

Comet was kept under close observation and in an oxygen tent for the remainder of the night and the following day. "When I was allowed to see him in his little tent, he started purring and I knew that was a good sign," Perry said.

On the second day, the kitten was released from the clinic. Said Perry, "He is totally back to his old self and just as adventurous as ever."

Well, that was a *clothes* call.

HEAD CASES

Two dogs—Lana and Luna—stuck their noses where they didn't belong and needed their heads examined. Literally.

In Riverside County, California, Lana, a three-month-old Australian cattle dog, liked to snoop around the neighborhood. But one day in 2020 she got her head stuck in the wheel of a spare tire that had been left outside by a garage. She had poked her head through the hole on a wheel that attaches to the hub on a truck's suspension. No one saw how she did it, but they could see she needed help because she couldn't free herself. She was a small dog in a large wheel.

Her owner, Martin Godinez, summoned Riverside County Animal Services, which dispatched a team. "It was so worrying to me," animal care technician David Hough told CNN. "I was trying to imagine how the heck she got put in that position, and you just got to remember that puppies will be puppies. Just curiosity. There was probably food on the other side of it or something, and she just crammed her head right through."

Hough and Animal Services officer Jose Cisneros used oil to lubricate the neck of the wriggly puppy. But they stopped trying to pull her head out when they noticed her neck was beginning to swell. With her head still stuck in the *wheel of misfortune*, they transported her to the Coachella Valley Animal Campus where Lana was sedated to calm her.

Where there's a wheel, there's a way, so firefighters from Riverside County Fire came to assist in the rescue. They took turns operating a reciprocating saw—a mechanical device used to free trapped victims in crashes—to cut a piece out of the wheel and safely removed Lana.

"She's totally fine now," Hough told CNN at the time. "She doesn't look fazed by it at all."

The headstrong puppy was back with the Godinez family, where she rested after her tiring ordeal.

Two years earlier, another dog, a brown mutt named Luna, ended up headfirst in a predicament.

Luna didn't exactly run into a brick wall, but she did get her head stuck in one.

"I started calling her outside and she never came," her owner, Kerri Foust, of Manteca, California, told Sacramento TV station KOVR. "I thought she got out or chased a cat over the wall." Foust eventually spotted Luna's rear end through some vegetation by the base of a brick wall surrounding the backyard. "I kept calling and I saw her tail wag," Foust said.

But the dog still wasn't coming to her. Only when Foust walked up to Luna did she realize why. The dog had poked her head through a hole in the wall and couldn't free herself.

"She was getting scared, and there was no way her head was coming out of that hole," Foust said. "I tried to put soap and water around her neck, but that didn't work."

Seeing the handwriting on the wall, Foust called 911. "We've had very much the traditional cat stuck in a tree, and we have had ducklings stuck in sewer drains," said firefighter Joshua Burke of the Lathrop-Manteca Fire District. But the department had never been called to rescue a *wall-eyed* pooch. "We get every kind of call you can possibly imagine and all the ones that you're never going to think of."

Rather than use the *paws* . . . oops . . . jaws of life to free the dog, firefighters placed a metal bar between Luna's head and the wall. Then, striking the bar with a sledgehammer, they chiseled the hole big enough to liberate the dog. The hole was then covered up.

A checkup at the animal clinic confirmed that Luna was fine. She probably just wanted to forget about her distress. But whenever she was in the backyard, she couldn't help but be reminded of the wall of shame.

DRY SPELLS

In two separate cases, cats tumbled in a near dead heat in clothes dryers.

Jasper the kitten proved to be such a hotshot for his dry run that he was nominated for the 2019 Hambone Award, an honor given out by Nationwide pet insurance for the year's strangest claim.

The family cat was watching owner Chelsey Yarbrough and her four children do the laundry in their house in Leander, Texas. "It was an unusually busy night," Yarbrough told Nationwide. "My girls are very sweet, and they often ask to help me out with laundry. They took the clothes from the washing machine and placed them into the dryer.

"Typically, I always check their work before I start the cycle." But on this night, everyone was distracted. No one realized that Jasper, who was in search of a nice dark place to snuggle in for the night, had vaulted inside the open dryer. Moments later, Yarbrough closed the dryer door and began dealing with one of her children who was upset and in tears over a disagreement with a sibling.

A short while later, "I heard some thumping and I was like, 'That's odd,'" Yarbrough recalled. "I was thinking maybe the kids threw a shoe in there or something crazy. Thankfully, I opened the door . . . and there he was." Jasper had been flopping around in the running dryer and now he was hot off the perma press.

The kitten, who was suffering from hyperthermia (overheating), was rushed to Central Texas Veterinary

Specialty and Emergency in nearby Austin. Vets worked feverishly to lower the kitten's extremely high fever. Kept overnight for treatment and observation, Jasper had no serious injuries from his wild ride and was released the next day.

If nothing else, the kitten gave new meaning to the term *dry cleaning*.

A year earlier, Holly, a six-year-old domestic shorthair, had a similar experience that left her hot under the collar.

Holly lived with her owner, Shelley Dorris, in Indianapolis along with four other cats and two dogs. With so many pets in the house, sometimes finding the right place for a good snooze wasn't easy, so, one day in 2018, Holly headed for the laundry room.

That same day, Dorris was multitasking while putting laundry into the front-loading dryer and didn't see Holly hop in with the wet clothes. Dorris closed the dryer door, turned on the dial, and left the room. She soon noticed that the dryer was making a strange noise as if it was off balance or had too many clothes in it.

"I opened the door and saw a little bit of her fur and her tail mixed in with the clothes," Dorris told Pet Pals TV. "And it was the worst feeling, a heart-wrenching feeling. I knew I needed to get her out, but I was afraid to see what I would find."

Holly was still alive but disoriented and suffering from hyperthermia. Dorris rushed Holly to Noah's Animal Hospital where the cat was given an IV to stabilize her. Among the issues the vets were worried about were possible organ failure and blood clots. But Holly survived. Dorris now has a magnet with a picture of Holly on her dryer to remind her to double-check before she closes the door and turns the dial. She didn't want Holly or any of her other cats to become hot and bothered.

BIRD BRAINED

Birds with a love for Indian cuisine had several embarrassing cooking mishaps. Usually when a person does something mortifying, he or she turns bright red. What these shameful birds did, however, left them turning bright orange.

A seagull, who was later nicknamed Gullfrazie, was flying by a food factory in Wales when he spotted a worker tossing out a substandard batch of curry into a small outdoor waste vat. Normally the tub was covered, but on this day in 2016, it wasn't. Because the seagull was hungry and liked curry, he flew down for a bird's-eye view. Perched on the thin edge of the vat, Gullfrazie decided to bob for pieces of that delicious Indian chicken.

But seagulls' webbed feet aren't designed to rest on

extremely thin objects. When Gullfrazie leaned over, he tumbled into the thick, orange concoction. Workers fished him out and rushed him to the Vale Wildlife Hospital in nearby Tewkesbury, Gloucestershire, England.

"He was bright orange when they brought him to us," veterinary nurse Lucy Kells told WalesOnline. "Half the staff thought he smelled fantastic and half thought he smelled awful. To me, he smelled delicious."

Those who liked the aroma of tikka masala—a favorite dish in the United Kingdom—made jokes about wanting to eat the bird. "When he came in, you wanted to feel sorry and concerned for him," Kells said. "But he was making everyone's belly rumble."

The staff, which named him Gullfrazie after a take on the Indian dish jalfrezi, used soap and water to clean him up although the smell of curry remained on him. "He was easy to clean because he had not been in the vat long, so the turmeric [a spice that gives the dish an orange color] hadn't had time to stain the feathers," Kells said. "Once we had got all the chicken tikka off him, he was looking quite nice."

She said the bird wasn't hurt, but he was a bit embarrassed. "He would normally have been able to take off after falling in the vat, but the curry was too thick and gloppy," she said. "He would have drowned had they not found him in there in time."

Gullfrazie remained in the hospital for several days while the natural oils on his feathers slowly returned. Staff fed him meat, dog food and cat food, and pieces of chopped fish to build up his weight. Not surprisingly, Kells said, "He does not like spicy food anymore."

Gullfrazie was eventually released to the wild. "We have had wildlife covered in cooking fat and glue, but we have never had one covered in curry before," Kells said. "It was the weirdest thing we have dealt with here."

It became less weird when, a few months later, another seagull with a taste for Indian food dove into a vat of orange tandoori sauce in a Newport, South Wales, food processing plant and had to be rescued. Its feathers dyed in bright orange, the bird was brought to the Vale Wildlife Hospital where staffers washed it and then set it free. "He was uninjured and just needed a good clean," a spokeswoman told the BBC. "But I expect he will be put off from curry after this."

Birds of a feather apparently do stick together, at least when it comes to Indian food. In 2019, a bright orange herring gull covered in vindaloo curry was spotted walking alongside an expressway and taken to Tiggywinkles Wildlife Hospital in Haddenham, Buckinghamshire, England. Staffers nicknamed him Vinny (after vindaloo).

"He had somehow gotten himself covered in curry or turmeric!" a post read on the hospital's Facebook page. "It was all over his feathers, preventing him from flying properly. We have no idea how he got into this predicament, but thankfully, apart from the vibrant color and pungent smell, he was healthy."

It seems that spicy Indian food truly is for the birds.

RABBIT STEW

A wirehaired dachshund named Ralph learned all about black holes. But that was a sore subject for him because he was trapped in a rabbit warren for five dark days.

"He does like chasing rabbits, and he does that a lot, but he just took it too far this time," his owner, Sarah McLellan, of Haworth, West Yorkshire, England, told the British newspaper *Metro* in 2019.

While on a walk with his four-legged sister, Edie, and their owner, Ralph caught a whiff of a rabbit and shot off, disappearing into the brush. When he didn't return, McLellan and her husband searched the area for days and even enlisted the aid of volunteers, including some who turned to social media for help. But there was no sign of Ralph.

They didn't know that the dachshund had followed a bunny into a rabbit hole that led five feet down into a maze of tunnels so small that he became stuck. During his *hare*-raising experience, the terrified dog tried digging his way out but made things much worse because the dirt collapsed around him, forcing him to wriggle into another rabbit run.

Meanwhile, McLellan was getting increasingly frantic, wondering if she would ever see her beloved pooch again. On the fifth day of Ralph's disappearance, her husband was on a walk with Edie about a half mile from home when Edie caught a scent and led him to a grassy area.

"At first my husband heard a dog whimpering," McLellan said. Hoping it might be Ralph, he summoned a friend who brought two shovels. Together they began carefully digging.

"Ralph was about five feet down, and they had to dig around him so the hole didn't collapse," she said. "It took them two hours.

"The rabbit holes are like mazes, and he must have gone through one hole and got stuck. He had made himself a hole in the middle, but he couldn't get out."

Guided by Ralph's whining, the two men finally freed him. "When he got out of the hole, he went for a wee," she said. "Then Ralph carried on as if nothing had happened."

Despite not eating for five days and nearly suffocating, Ralph didn't suffer any serious health issues while trapped in the hole. "He is completely knackered [exhausted], and he has worn down his nails from when he was trying to dig himself out," McLellan said. "But he is otherwise fine. He's lost weight and he's so tired. He just needs time to build himself back up again.

"It was such a drama and I was still in shock when I saw him. I was up until 1 a.m. last night just cuddling him. Hopefully, he has learned his lesson this time."

No doubt Ralph became fed up with the *hole* ordeal.

AN ARRESTING DEVELOPMENT

A raccoon thought he had found the perfect place to steal some snacks—by sneaking inside a school's vending machine. That was the easy part. The hard part was the getaway.

One afternoon in 2019, the masked bandit slipped inside Pine Ridge High School in Deltona, Florida. When no one was looking, he jumped up into the tray of the vending machine and gained access inside by going through the swinging flap. Because it was in a school, he probably was looking for *academia nuts*, *apple chips*, or *pop arts*.

Everything was going according to plan. He could have his pick of as many packaged snacks as he wanted. And they wouldn't cost him anything. At least, that's what he assumed.

He didn't realize that he would, indeed, pay a price for his shenanigans.

Rather than eat his snacks inside the machine, he thought it would be best if he brought them back to his den. But when he tried to leave, he discovered that the flap only moved in one direction—inward and not outward.

He was trapped. Because the front of the machine was glass, the criminal critter was totally exposed. Students wanting granola bars turned to snickers when they saw a raccoon staring back at them, so deputies from the Volusia County Sheriff's Office were called to the scene. But they couldn't arrest the bandit without first getting him out of his predicament. Before doing anything, they snapped a few incriminating photos of the raccoon who was wedged underneath some Herr's potato chips and above the Welch's Fruit Snacks.

Accompanying a social media post of the pictures, the sheriff's office said, "This gentleman was apprehended today while committing a burglary of a vending machine at Pine Ridge High School."

Deputy Danny Clifton summoned Deltona Animal Control Officer Marion Quinones. They put the vending machine on a dolly and wheeled it outside the school. Then they made the raccoon a deal he couldn't refuse: Leave the loot behind and he could go free. They opened the back of the machine, and, with a prod from a pole, they convinced him to take the offer. Said the sheriff's office, "Our friend [made] his exit to freedom. He did so with a little encouragement, and he's off to his next adventure."

The raccoon decided against any further extracurricular *snacktivity*.

VANDALS

TROUBLED WATERS

Eve the cat got into hot water by flooding her owners' new home, causing about $25,000 in damage.

Spending what would become a memorable night in the laundry room in 2020, Eve was a little bored, so she began playing with the spigot that, when connected and turned on, provided water to the washing machine. Batting the lever back and forth, the one-year-old Bengal eventually turned the tap to full blast. For hours and hours, a steady stream gushed from the spigot, flooding the entire downstairs.

When owners Joe and Amber Fauser of Adelaide, South Australia, left Eve in the laundry room for the night, they had no idea that their impish cat was trying to destroy their comfy home. *Water* surprise it was when they woke up the next morning.

"My husband and I went to bed at about 10 p.m., and we had put Eve in the laundry room to sleep, as we have done for the past year," Amber told Adelaide's 7NEWS. "Around 6 a.m. the next morning, Joe woke up for work and was greeted by water almost at our door."

At first mystified by all the water, he ran throughout the house, searching for the source of the flood. He found it when he entered the laundry room. There, sitting on top of the washing machine as though this cool cat didn't have a care in the world, was Eve.

"We knew it was Eve straight away," said Amber. "She is always causing havoc and playing with things because the Bengal in her makes her super curious."

Joe shut off the water and picked up Eve and put her in another room where she couldn't cause any trouble because he didn't want her to go from one ex-*stream* to another. He then called his boss to say he wouldn't be showing up for work because, well, there was water under the fridge and most everywhere else on the first floor.

As memories of that watery wake-up call came flooding back, Amber said, "We hired a flood emergency services team. It took the whole day for them to suck up as much excess water as possible. They ripped up our floorboards and some of our carpet and placed thirty different dryers and dehumidifiers in the house, which stayed on for seven days and made our electricity bill skyrocket."

After contacting their insurance company and hiring local tradesmen, the pair learned how much damage their little cat had done: nearly $40,000 in Australian dollars (about $31,000 U.S. dollars). "We had moved into our new house only three months prior, so we did whatever we had to do to save it," Amber said. Nearly half the cost was for drying out the home and the electricity bill for the fans and dehumidifiers. The residence was quickly repaired.

"To make sure this doesn't happen again, we bought child safety locks," said Amber. "And we aren't letting Eve into the laundry room anymore."

BACK SCRATCHER

Vitus the donkey relished fancy automobiles. And that was a problem because he gnawed on the rear of an extremely expensive sports car, causing thousands of dollars in damages.

Like many people, Vitus couldn't help but admire the $356,000 bright orange McLaren Spider 650S convertible that Markus Zahn drove around Vogelsberg, Germany, in 2016. Vitus had the opportunity to view the car up close one day when Zahn backed up the luxury vehicle and parked it next to the donkey's fenced-in paddock.

Zahn then walked away, failing to notice Vitus strolling toward the Spider. That car was so appetizing to the donkey that he could just taste it. And that's exactly what he did. Although a wood rail and wire fence separated Vitus from the car, the animal squeezed his head through the barrier and licked the back of the vehicle. Then he took a bite. And another one. To Vitus, fine dining was enjoying a super-pricey sports car.

When Zahn returned, he glanced briefly at Vitus without realizing that the donkey was savoring the moment. The businessman hopped into his sports car and then gasped. "I looked in the rearview mirror and suddenly saw a pair of fluffy ears," he told the German newspaper *Bild*. "And then I heard a strange sound. The sound was the donkey gnawing on my fender." Zahn leaped out of the car and surveyed the damage. The high-priced paint job—Elite Volcano Orange—was now marred by teeth marks and scratches. Vitus also tried to munch on the carbon fiber spoiler that was attached to the rear. The total damage: $37,000.

So why did Vitus want to eat the Spider? "The motive to the crime is still completely unclear," local police said in a statement. "It was not possible to get more than a 'heehaw' out of him."

Zahn had a theory: "The donkey probably thought the car was a carrot on wheels. Yes, he obviously thought he had stumbled upon a giant carrot." He added, "I'm not mad at him."

But Zahn was mad at the donkey's owner, who refused to pay for any of the damages because, he claimed, the businessman should have known better than to park next to the paddock. Zahn sued, and in 2017, the regional court in Giessen ruled that Vitus's owner had to pony up more than $6,000 for the damages not covered by insurance.

As for all the trouble Vitus had caused, he didn't seem to *carrot* all.

ALL FIRED UP

A French bulldog–Boston terrier mix used to be called Archie. But after what he did to an apartment, he earned a more descriptive name: Archie the Arsonist.

Shortly after his owner, Danielle Danski, of East Melbourne, Australia, left her residence for a workout in the gym one morning in 2019, the 10-month-old pup found a barbecue grill lighter and figured it would make a dandy chew toy. With the lighter in his mouth, Archie hopped onto the living room couch and began gnawing away.

Even though the lighter had a safety lock on it, Archie managed to disengage it. He obviously didn't know how *fireworks*. Suddenly, the lighter shot out a flame that ignited a blanket that was draped over the couch. In a flash, the couch caught fire, spurring Archie to flee the room.

Meanwhile, Danski, who had no idea that her home was on fire, decided to check on Archie by using an app on her phone that displayed a live feed from her closed-circuit TV security camera. She was shocked when she saw that her couch was engulfed in flames. Danski immediately alerted the Metropolitan Fire Brigade (MFB), which arrived on the scene within three minutes and extinguished the blaze, but not before it caused extensive damage estimated at the equivalent of $40,000 in U.S. dollars. The other apartments were not affected.

"The fire completely ravaged my home, all of the contents of the room, as well as the walls, cupboard, and air conditioner," Danski told Australian TV's 10NewsFirst.

Luckily, Archie was not hurt. "Little Archie was in the other room, scared to death," Danski's mother, Eva, told 9News. "She rushed him to the vet to have his lungs checked, but he was fine. All he needed was a big wash because he was covered in soot."

Eva said if she hadn't seen the video from the security camera, she never would have believed the dog could have set the place on fire. "I can't even start [the lighter] very well," she added. "I don't know how he managed to do it."

MFB Commander Graeme O'Sullivan said he was stunned that the pooch could start a fire with a lighter. "I've never seen anything like that in thirty years on the job," he said.

"We've had a few calls in the past where dogs and cats have knocked over candles, incense, or oil burners, but this is certainly the first time we've seen a fire caused in this fashion.

"It's a little bit of a funny story, but I guess the main message is just for people to make sure to store those items safely because this just goes to show what can happen."

He said that when Danski showed up at the scene of the fire, Archie ran and jumped in her arms, adding, "I think he knew he'd done something wrong and was in a bit of trouble."

Danski said she was willing to forgive her pet, who had his own Instagram page for several months before the blaze. However, she changed his Instagram name to "Archie the Arsonist," and captioned a photo of the firebug with "We've had a *ruff* week."

When Kahuna the dog noticed a bunch of items sitting on an ironing board, he had a pressing need to examine them up close. He clumsily knocked everything over and soon created a hot mess by setting the house on fire.

The nine-month-old mutt and his older canine buddy, Paige, were home alone in Los Alamos, New Mexico, while their owner was at work one day in 2020. Paige was snoozing on the floor in the living room when Kahuna's interest in the ironing board was sparked by all the things that their owner had left on it.

A home security camera shows what happened next: Kahuna hopped onto an ottoman that was next to the ironing board. Standing on his hind legs, he put his front paws on the ironing board and sniffed at a backpack, an unplugged iron, and other items. As he leaned in for a closer look, he tipped over the ironing board, which crashed to the floor, along with all the other items, in a loud bang.

Freaked out, Kahuna sprinted over to the nearby couch, turned around, and stared at the problem he caused while poor Paige was jolted awake from her slumber. Paige went over to the overturned ironing board and then looked at Kahuna, who was still frozen on the couch as if telling himself, "How am I going to iron out this bad situation?"

This bad situation was about to get inflamed. The items had fallen on top of a heating vent on the floor, which wouldn't have been such a big deal if the furnace below wasn't operating. Unfortunately, it was.

According to a news release from the Los Alamos Fire Department: "The furnace produced sufficient heat to melt some items, which flowed [through the floor grate] into the heater and served as the necessary fuel to initiate the fire down inside the furnace unit."

About an hour after Kahuna knocked over the ironing board, flames began shooting up from the floor vent. That was Kahuna's cue to leave the room. Paige, on the other hand, seemed clueless as she lounged on the couch. As security video shows, she casually looks around the room and then jerks in surprise when she finally discovers the corner of the room is on fire. She walks toward the blaze and then, realizing that this is not good, waddles out of the room as though out of sight, out of mind.

Firefighters soon arrived to snuff out the fire before it damaged the whole house. The dogs were safe and unharmed. Said the release, "LAFD recommends that combustible items not be placed on or within three feet of heating devices, especially when pets are left home alone and could knock items onto the heaters." As for Kahuna, he's now the star of a video on what a pet shouldn't do.

The news release added that Kahuna "declined to comment but is expected to enroll in dog training classes for fire prevention soon." Well, the dog had to take some heat for causing the fire.

SCARE BEAR

A black bear vandalized a beached kayak, nearly stranding the owner in the Alaskan wilderness.

The bruin faced off with adventurer Mary Maley, who was on the fifth day of a planned three-week solo kayaking trip in 2015. She had paddled to shore in Berg Bay, 22 miles southeast of the town of Wrangell, to rest in a remote U.S. Forest Service cabin. Maley had brought in her tent, food, and gear but left her kayak by the water's edge. As she ate lunch, she heard a noise and went outside to see a disturbing sight. A bear was chomping on her $4,000 kayak. She yelled at him to scram, but he ignored her at first.

Maley grabbed her pepper spray and camera, walked out of the cabin, and began recording the encounter, which she later shared on YouTube. In the video, the bear stops wrecking the boat and ambles toward Maley, who says, "Thanks for leaving my kayak alone." The bear moves closer to her, prompting her to warn him, "I'm going to pepper spray you in the face." Apparently, he doesn't believe her until she pepper sprays him in the face.

It stops the bruin momentarily. If he had any intention of running off into the woods, he's changed his mind.

Now it is all about revenge. Returning to the kayak, he gives Maley a quick stare of contempt and begins pawing and gnawing on her kayak again. "Bear! Bear! Bear! You're breaking my kayak!" Maley shouts. "Why are you doing that? Why are you breaking my kayak?" she asks repeatedly. "What am I going to do? Stop it!"

It is obvious at this point that the bruin doesn't understand English. He continues to vandalize her boat as it bears the brunt of his anger. With her voice rising in pitch, the stressed-out woman screams, "Bear, stop it! Stop it, bear! Please stop! Gosh darn it! Oh!" He is now ripping up her seat and back support. "It's the end of September. You are supposed to be asleep. Why are you here?"

Well, because there is a kayak to ravage, and, besides, bears answer questions with their teeth and claws. Other than Yogi and Smokey, bears don't actually talk.

Maley repeatedly cries, "Bear, stop that!" Her voice keeps going higher as she pleads, "Please stop breaking my things!"

The furry vandal then flips the kayak over and chomps on it. "It's not food," she yells. "It doesn't even taste good. [Not that she ever tasted a kayak before.] It's just plastic!"

The two-and-a-half-minute video, which ends with the bear still trashing the kayak, has more than five and a half million views. Among the comments:

- "Of course he's not gonna listen. She keeps calling him Bear when his name is actually Steve."
- "The world's most interesting bear: 'I don't always get pepper sprayed, but when I do, I dismantle kayaks.'"
- "She said 'bear' 31 times. That's gotta be a record."
- "Today I learned that incessant nagging, no matter how heartfelt, is not a good bear deterrent."
- "What was worse? The pepper spray? Or her incessant 'bear' screaming? Poor bear. Probably in therapy right now."

Maley said the bear continued to batter the kayak for another ten minutes after she had stopped shooting video. After he wandered off, Maley dragged her badly damaged kayak up to the cabin. Seeing a sailboat anchored in the bay, she swam out to it and told the sailors her hard-luck tale. They brought Maley, her gear, and kayak to Wrangell where she patched up the gashes. But even with the repairs, it was not safe to take the boat back out in the wilderness, so she ended her trip.

As for the bear, well, he learned that *you can't have your kayak and eat it, too.*

A rogue squirrel ransacked the inside of a house while its owners were on vacation, causing thousands of dollars in damage.

Dustin and Kari Drees had just purchased their first home in December 2019—a cute cottage-style residence in the Atlanta suburb of Buckhead. For the holidays, the couple and their one-year-old daughter flew to San Diego to visit relatives.

While they were gone, an alarm went off in their house. The security firm that monitored the alarm dispatched a service person who found no signs of forced entry. The following day, the alarm sounded again. "This time, we had a friend check it out," Kari told Atlanta TV station WSB. "Our doors and windows were intact, so we just thought it was a software issue."

There was an issue all right. But it wasn't from a glitch. It was from a destructive rodent who had either tumbled or crawled down the chimney of the unoccupied home, and then went completely nutso when it couldn't find its way out.

It left a trail of sooty pawprints from the fireplace through every room of the house. Furniture, including a new couch, was soiled. The scoundrel chewed on wooden windowsills, shutters, doors, window frames, and even baseboards. It scratched the polished wood floors and poked tiny holes in the windows. In its mad but futile effort to escape, it turned on the faucet on the kitchen sink, causing hot tap water to run for days and days. And the squirrel pooped everywhere, leaving droppings on the kitchen counter, the floor, the couple's bed, and their couch.

"He ran across the couch, ran through the dining room. He even went in the bathroom, somehow got in the toilet, and then went in our daughter's room," Dustin told the *Washington Post*. "He was just trying to figure a way out of the house."

The couple didn't know any of this until they returned from their trip and discovered their house was in shambles. At first, they thought a vandal or burglar had ravaged their home. But the evidence pointed to one culprit: The home-wrecker was a squirrel. Then it dawned on them that the rodent might still be in the house.

They were right. The trespasser was hiding in their favorite piece of furniture—the couch. "He made a little bed in there," Dustin said. "It's a comfy couch." The couple called a critter control company that sent a technician who found the squirrel quivering behind a couch pillow. When its hiding place was discovered, the squirrel freaked out and went rogue again, scrambling here and there before it was finally captured and removed, according to Dustin.

The next day, workers wearing hazmat suits cleaned the house and placed "sanitation bombs" in every room at a cost of $2,000. The squirrel ended up causing more than $15,000 in damages. To make matters worse for the couple, their homeowner's insurance didn't cover any of the expenses to replace everything that got gnawed.

Moaned Kari, "It's hard to believe a little tiny squirrel could do this much damage." Hmm, sounds like she was *critter sizing* the rodent.

THE DARK SIDE

In 2014, squirrels launched an all-out attack against the Cincinnati Zoo & Botanical Garden's annual month-long holiday celebration. The bushy-tailed vandals kept gnawing on strands of lights, darkening sections of the PNC Festival of Lights, an event that attracts about 250,000 people to the zoo during Christmastime.

The rodents should have been thankful to hang out at the zoo, considering they had plenty of trees for their nests and all the water, young plants, and discarded food, like pizza crust and peanuts, they could possibly want. Also keep in mind that their nearest predators were all in cages or enclosures. And yet, when it came to the holiday lights, these ungrateful squirrels gave a collective "Bah humbug!"

Before the holiday season, the zoo strung about two million lights on strands shielded in plastic—a type of plastic that the squirrels found quite appetizing. So when the zoo closed down for the evening, the rodents had themselves a buffet, chewing on the strands. To the furry miscreants, it was a light workout.

Each morning the groundskeepers checked the lights and had to replace all the strands that had been chewed through. They even put hot sauce on some of the strands to discourage the rascals. But that didn't work. Who knew that the squirrels liked to eat electrical cords with a dash of spicy sauce?

The groundskeepers were aware that the squirrels also love tulip bulbs. Brian Jorg, manager of the zoo's native plant program, told the *Cincinnati Enquirer* that the zoo plants 105,000 tulip bulbs each year, and though they're covered in plastic netting, those squirrelly rascals manage to dig up thousands of them.

Jorg said when he wants 100 oak seedlings to grow, he plants 500 of them because he expects he will lose 80 percent to the squirrels. He said, "When you are becoming a horticulturist, you never [are told] that a rodent will be the bane of your existence."

It's obvious that those darn squirrels at the zoo like to make flower *derangements*.

CHOWHOUNDS

MONEY HUNGRY

Ozzie the labradoodle put his money where his mouth was, except it wasn't his money. It was his owners'. And he didn't just put it in his mouth. He ate it. Two hundred dollars' worth.

His owners, Neil and Judith Wright, of Llandudno, North Wales, had gone out shopping and left their nine-year-old dog alone in the house one day in 2019. Someone had owed the couple the equivalent of $200, so the person put eight £20 notes in a pink plastic bank bag and slipped it through a mail slot in the front door.

When Ozzie spotted it, he had more money than sense. Unable to spend it, he munched his way through the bag and tore into the cash. When the couple returned home, they found pieces of banknotes scattered throughout the hallway and into the kitchen. One look at the guilt on Ozzie's face, and they knew they had a cash flow problem.

"We have had Ozzie since he was a pup and he has been known to eat other items before, but never money," Judith told the *Daily Mirror*. "I phoned the person who had posted it through the door to ask how much money it was."

Based on what was left of the chewed-up money, the couple realized that Ozzie had swallowed a significant sum, so they brought him to Murphy & Co Veterinary Practice where the canine fool and his money were soon parted by making him vomit. The dog threw up dirty money, pieces of the bank bag, and a money clip.

It was a pricey meal. In addition to the $200 Ozzie chewed up, it cost the Wrights another $160 for the vet bill to retrieve the remnants of the banknotes. However, the Bank of England reimbursed the couple about $100 worth of banknotes that were more than half intact. The Wrights also put a cage on the mail slot to catch the mail so Ozzie could no longer get to it.

They didn't want their dog to be a *mail chauvinist pig*.

HARD TO SWALLOW

Acting as though they were sword swallowers, dogs in two separate cases needed emergency surgery after wolfing down kebabs that were still on the skewers.

One day in 2019, Marmite, an 11-year-old cocker spaniel, noticed that his owner, Sharon Brown, of Moreton Morrell, Warwickshire, England, had tossed into the kitchen garbage can two leftover half-eaten chicken kebabs that were on 10-inch wooden skewers.

Late that night, Marmite went into the kitchen, opened the lid to the garbage can, and started to help himself to the kebabs. Unfortunately, he swallowed much more than he could chew.

"I went into the kitchen at around 11 p.m. and saw Marmite swallowing something as quickly as possible," Brown told the British newspaper *Metro*. "I noticed the bin [garbage can] was open and I knew straight away he'd helped himself to the leftovers of our kebab take-away [takeout]. Within five or ten minutes, he was clearly in trouble. He was gagging, trying to stretch out from tip to toe, and was wobbly and falling over."

She rushed him to the Avonvale Veterinary Centre in Warwick where he underwent emergency surgery. Recalled veterinary surgeon Elly McPhee, "The first thing we did was put a video camera down Marmite's esophagus," which connects the throat to the stomach. "Halfway down we found a chicken kebab complete with a long, wooden skewer. There were even chicken and peppers still attached to it, so he had obviously swallowed it whole.

"It was lodged hard and we were unable to retrieve it, which is why Marmite needed an emergency operation. The only possible way of removing the kebab was by going into the stomach and pulling it down, through the esophagus and finally out. However, as soon I'd gone into the stomach, I realized there was a second kebab and skewer lodged in there, too, so we ended up removing both."

Marmite made a complete recovery.

"The vets were brilliant," said Brown. "They were all heroes. When I went in to see Marmite after the operation, they showed me the two kebabs that they had removed. It was amazing. I'd obviously caught him in the act, and he'd just gobbled them down as quickly as possible without even chewing them."

You might say that Hoshi, a six-year-old Shar-Pei, wasn't the sharpest utensil in the kitchen drawer. But then again, maybe she was the sharpest—at least for the moment in 2018 when she swallowed an entire chicken kebab that was on an eight-inch metal skewer.

The dog was at a barbecue in Glasgow, Scotland, when she noticed that several chicken kebabs were left unattended by the grill. Seizing her chance, she snatched one of the kebabs and downed it before anyone saw her do it.

The chicken might have tasted fine but consuming a metal skewer was awful. Hoshi was in pain and had a lump in her side—you could call it a sore spot—so her owner, Sandra Kin, took her to the Roundhouse Veterinary Hospital where X-rays were taken.

"We were astounded when X-rays revealed that the swelling on Hoshi's abdomen was the point of a large metal skewer piercing her ribs, which she had apparently swallowed at the barbecue," veterinary surgeon Ruth Greening told the BBC. Greening operated on Hoshi and removed the skewer. The dog, who spent three days in the hospital, made a complete recovery.

Said Kin, "Hoshi's a little bit crazy, but I guess that's why we love her."

The skewer episode is beside the point.

RING-A-DING-A-LING

A goldendoodle puppy named Bella admired her owner's wedding ring so much she ate it.

Cindy McCombs of Ada, Michigan, woke up one morning in 2018 and discovered that her custom-designed combination wedding and engagement ring was missing. After she and her husband Dan looked everywhere without any luck, they wondered if Bella had turned into a jewelry thief. After all, she liked to grab things off tables and hide them in the yard.

Dan borrowed a metal detector and waved it through the house and around the yard, but the device didn't detect anything. Not until he casually swept it over Bella's stomach did the detector buzz. It could mean only one thing: Bella had swallowed the ring.

The couple took her to Thornwood Veterinary Clinic in Ada, where an X-ray confirmed their suspicions. On the vet's recommendation, Bella was brought to BluePearl Veterinary Partners in nearby Grand Rapids because it specialized in internal medicine and surgery.

The staff tried to get Bella to vomit, hoping she would cough up the ring, but that effort didn't work. Because the couple wanted to avoid surgery for the dog, Dr. Kristopher Sharpe decided to use special forceps, an instrument that has miniature claws to grasp objects in the stomach. After putting Bella under anesthesia, Sharpe inserted the device down her throat and into her stomach, where he was able to grasp the ring and pull it out.

Twenty minutes after the procedure, Bella woke up and was soon wagging her tail. Like the dog, the wedding ring was in good shape after the procedure, reported Grand Rapids TV station WZZM. "We were all very relieved to get this done without surgery," Sharpe said. "It was a good outcome, and getting the ring back makes it even better."

The veterinarian said he had retrieved a variety of objects in pets' stomachs such as socks, toys, and even a spoon. But a wedding ring? That was a first, which makes Bella a *ringleader.*

Three years earlier, another dog—a black Labrador retriever puppy named Sierra—also developed an expensive taste in jewelry. She swallowed her owner's engagement ring and wedding band worth $23,000.

"I saw my dogs, Sierra and Tahoe, near the coffee table and remembered I'd left my rings sitting on the table the previous night," Stephanie Lamb of Tulsa, Oklahoma, told local TV station KOKI. "By the time I ran over there, the two rings were gone. I knew it was Sierra because she's just a little bit of a troublemaker."

Lamb brought Sierra to Southern Hills Veterinary Hospital where the dog was x-rayed and examined by Dr. Rodney Robards, who decided surgery was needed.

He told KOKI that waiting for the rings to come out naturally would have been a risky option because they could have damaged her intestines.

The operation on the bauble-bellied dog was successful. Dr. Robards was able to retrieve both the diamond ring and the wedding band. Unfortunately, the wedding band was bent out of shape. During the surgery, he discovered Sierra's appetite went beyond jewelry. "She eats more than rings, I'm afraid," he told the TV station. "There were some rocks in there and some sticks or maybe bones."

Well, at least this story has a nice ring to it.

WITHIN EARSHOT

Eddie the emu caused his handler to suffer severe earring loss. He pecked her expensive diamond earrings right off her earlobes.

The young bird arrived as an orphan at Kobble Bird Shelter in Brisbane, Australia, in 2018 after his father was run over in western Queensland. Wildlife supervisor Melanie Pope was caring for Eddie, and the two formed a close bond. As she did most every day, Pope wore her $2,000 diamond earrings.

"He's attracted to anything shiny, and as I was picking him up to move him from inside to outside, he grabbed one of my earrings," she told the *Sunday Mail*. "He was lightning fast, and the back of the earring just dropped and fell to the floor. As I was trying to recover from the shock, he got the other one, too."

Pope took Eddie to the vet to determine if the emu might pass the jewels, but X-rays revealed they were in his gut and that surgery might be necessary if Eddie didn't poop them out.

"He's only a little bird and I didn't want him to go through the ordeal of an operation just for a pair of earrings, lovely as they were," she said.

After sifting through Eddie's poop for several days without finding the diamonds, Pope brought Eddie back to the animal hospital to have his stomach pumped in the hopes that the sparklies would come out in the end. But no such luck: just some stones, a piece of pottery, and a five-cent Australian coin.

Claiming her diamonds were *ear-replaceable*, she contacted her insurance company. Based on Eddie's X-rays, it agreed to cover the cost of the half-carat diamonds and white gold studs. "My insurance company was absolutely amazed when I told them what had happened and laughed pretty hard," she said. "They laughed even harder when they saw the X-rays."

As for Eddie, he had no ill effects from his ear-bending escapade. He was kept at the sanctuary for six months and then released into the wild. Said Pope, "Eddie has rocks in his head, not to mention his belly."

Vinnie the Chihuahua might have been the lovable mascot at a hair salon, but he also turned out to be an accessory to theft when he gulped down a $650 diamond earring.

Hairdressers Kevin and Gary Wightman, who ran a salon from their home in Dundee, Scotland, were mystified when one of their client's earrings went missing while her hair was being cut in 2017.

"The client always takes her earrings off and usually puts them in her purse while she's getting her hair done," Kevin told the *Evening Telegraph*. "But I think on this occasion she was busy chatting and just put them down on the waiting bench. When we were finished, there was only one earring there." Naturally, she was quite *ear-itated*.

"We've got two larger dogs, so we thought they had maybe wagged their tails and knocked the earring off," Kevin said. After a thorough search of the house, they couldn't find it.

However, they did uncover evidence that led them to believe Vinnie was responsible for the theft. They found the backing to the missing earring on the Chihuahua's bed. But there was still no sign of the diamond.

"I was convinced he hadn't swallowed it because he is really tiny," Kevin said. But just to make sure, they brought the dog to Parkside Vets where the staff induced him to throw up. Everything in his stomach came out except the diamond.

"They couldn't do anything else because Vinnie is so small, so we just had to keep an eye on him," said Kevin. "Two days later, I took him out at 7 a.m. and he went to do the toilet as usual. I got the flashlight out on my phone and I immediately knew the earring was there because it was sparkling in his poo."

After they cleaned the diamond, they returned it to their client who grinned earring to earring.

"We'll just have to keep a close eye on Vinnie in the future," said Kevin. "He's a wee menace, and he's always looking for the next thing to steal."

His owners will want to keep him out of *earring* distance.

ARMED TO THE TEETH

Benno took the expression "bite the bullet" way too literally. The son of a gun ate 22 live rounds of .308 caliber ammunition.

The Belgian Malinois chewed the bullets until he

had mangled them and then swallowed them one by one. Fortunately, he didn't shoot himself in the mouth.

The large four-year-old dog had been known to eat inedible things, so it wasn't surprising that he became locked and loaded in 2015. "You can baby-proof a house, but I don't think it's possible to Benno-proof a house," his owner, Larry "Sonny" Brassfield, of Mountain Home, Arkansas, told the local newspaper, *Baxter Bulletin*. "Lord knows, we've tried and failed."

One evening, Brassfield put several hundred rounds into ammunition cans. Because he didn't have enough cans, there were about 200 bullets left over. He tossed them in a bag, which he placed by his bed, knowing Benno had never shown any interest in ammo. Ah, but that night, Benno acted like a big shot and set his sights on those shiny bullets.

"The next morning, my wife said Benno had thrown up," Brassfield told the newspaper. "She said there was a bullet in the vomit. I looked at the round and I thought, 'Oh my God, he got into the ammo.'" The owner couldn't tell how many bullets Benno had consumed, so he watched his dog for a while. "He ate like he normally did, no problem," Brassfield recalled. "Then about fifteen to twenty minutes later, he threw up again and three more rounds came out. At that point, I knew I had to take him to the vet."

Brassfield brought Benno to All Creatures Animal Hospital where veterinarian Sarah Sexton examined the dog and took X-rays, which showed more than a dozen rounds in his stomach. "We learned in veterinary school there's what you read in the textbooks and there's what you see in the real world," she told the newspaper. "This kind of case is something they certainly did not cover in school. I've treated dogs that ate strange things before, mostly stuffed toys. But this takes the cake."

Unlike many bullets that are made of lead and zinc, which are highly toxic to dogs, the ammo that Benno ate was made from brass and copper, which aren't deadly. Still, Dr. Sexton needed to operate on the dog to remove the bullets. "There were lots of jokes being told during the surgery," she said. "He could have gone up in smoke or he could have gone out with a bang. Oh, there were lots of jokes."

During surgery, which lasted about two hours, the veterinarian removed 16 live, highly chewed rounds and one shell from the dog's stomach. "It was an adventure," she said.

After the successful operation, Dr. Sexton again x-rayed the dog and spotted two more rounds in his esophagus. The vet decided against further surgery, figuring that Benno would either vomit out the two remaining nontoxic bullets or poop them out. He passed one of them five days later and the other one after eight days.

"I won't be leaving ammunition laying around any-more, I can tell you that," Brassfield told the newspaper. "But, really, you're never going to stop him. It's just a question of what he's going to eat next."

In his first four years, Benno had eaten or chewed on the following: stuffed animals, rubber toys, coins, squares of cloth, Styrofoam peanuts, cheese wrappers, books, wax paper, aluminum foil, shirts, socks, under-wear, a bra, tennis shoes, rope, plastic weed trimmer string, a gasoline-soaked lawn mower air filter, blankets, marbles, straight pins, a plastic soda bottle, bottle lids, magnets, a television remote, a loaf of bread (includ-ing the wrapper), broken glass, chicken legs (swallowed whole), a nylon hairbrush, LEGOs, a travel-size bottle of lotion, parts of a baseboard, and a piece of a wall.

Hopefully Benno won't eat birthday candles, because you wouldn't want him to suffer from heartburn.

CHICKEN-HEARTED

Colbie the husky discovered that too much of a good thing was a bad thing.

In her case, it was chicken. Lots of chicken. Six

pounds of chicken—all at one time. Her chicken overdose led to emergency surgery and a nomination for "Most Unusual Claim of the Month" by Nationwide, the country's largest provider of pet health insurance.

The two-year-old dog was homeless until she joined the family of Youssef Saliba and Elizabeth Streb of Yucaipa, California, in 2018. "When we first saw Colbie, we thought she was crazy beautiful," Saliba told Nationwide, "We wanted to give her a chance at being a part of our family. We had her for two weeks before we chose to give her a forever home." Colbie fit right in and enjoyed going on hikes with the family. Like so many rescue dogs, she acted as though she never had enough to eat even though she was given a healthy amount.

One night the refrigerator stopped working, which the couple didn't discover until the next day, when it was too late to save the perishable food. Among the items thrown into the garbage can were six pounds of cooked chicken.

There is an old saying that goes, "One person's trash is another person's treasure." Colbie certainly believed in that message. While the couple was at work, Colbie, who had access to the backyard, picked up the scent of the tossed-out chicken. She went over to the trash can and knocked it over, causing the lid to open. Like a fox in a henhouse, she gorged herself on the chicken. Wings. Thighs. Breasts. Bones. It was *poultry in motion*. Even when her belly was full, the dog kept eating until there was nothing left to eat.

When Streb returned home, she expected Colbie to rush up and greet her as the husky normally did. But that didn't happen this time. "Elizabeth discovered Colbie lying on the ground next to the trash can, unable to move," Saliba recalled. "Elizabeth started to panic, unsure of what we had thrown inside the garbage can and what Colbie may have eaten."

Streb immediately took Colbie to the Emergency Pet Hospital of Redlands, hoping that it wasn't too late. The vets tried to induce Colbie to vomit, but she couldn't because she had consumed too much food. As a last resort, they performed an intestinal resection operation because all the chicken she had eaten was blocking her digestive system. That's when they discovered that Colbie had eaten up to six pounds of chicken and chicken bones. The surgery successfully cleared the blockage.

It took ten days of around-the-clock supervision before Colbie regained her normal health. Meanwhile, the couple took extra measures to make sure she wouldn't break into the trash can again. After all, they didn't want the dog to *fowl up*.

OFF HIS GAME

Rocco, a four-year-old Staffordshire bull terrier, took his video game to a whole new level—down inside his gut.

Yep, he swallowed a video game.

Owners Sean Johnston and Rebecca Moss of Cumbernauld, North Lanarkshire, Scotland, knew something was wrong in 2019 when Rocco started vomiting and refused to eat. Because his condition didn't improve, Johnston brought the dog to the Glasgow PDSA Shamrock Street Pet Hospital.

"Rocco was admitted immediately, and our vets were stunned when X-rays revealed a rectangular shaped object in his gut," according to a PDSA news release. "After rushing him into surgery to remove the potentially fatal object, they retrieved a video game cartridge lodged in his small intestine." It turned out to be a Nintendo DS cartridge.

"He wasn't acting himself at all, and we were worried he'd eaten a corn on the cob," Johnston said. "But we were so shocked when the vet said it was from a video game! We don't own a Nintendo or anything like that, so we're baffled as to where he got it from. He's a rescue dog and we've only had him for about six months, so the only thing we can think is that it was from his previous owners. Who knows how long it's been in there."

Left untreated, the cartridge could have caused a deadly blockage. In other words, it would have been game over for Rocco. "Our experienced surgeon was able to carry out the successful operation that same day, and after an overnight stay to keep a close eye on his recovery, Rocco was discharged the following day for rest and recovery," said the PDSA.

Added senior vet Susan Hermit, "We see dogs that eat strange things all the time, but none of us had ever seen anything like this."

At the time, Johnston said, "Even though we haven't had him that long, he's already such a big part of the family, so we're delighted to have him back home. He's made a brilliant recovery."

As for Rocco trying a new video game, here's a suggestion: *Nintendon't.*

TOUGH COOKIES

Marley, a seven-year-old Labrador retriever, admired his owner's handmade gingerbread Christmas tree decorations so much that he ate 34 of them, including the holiday ribbons that were attached to each one.

He wasn't a smart cookie, because his appetite nearly cost him his life.

The black lab had watched Rachel Bulmer of Bournemouth, Dorset, England, lovingly make the cookie decorations for her friends and family to put on their Christmas trees in 2019. She had tied green and gold ribbons onto each little gingerbread tree. After putting the decorations in gift bags, she placed them on the kitchen counter to give out later. Then she left the room.

While Bulmer was gone, Marley went back into the kitchen and gorged himself on nearly three dozen of the Christmas cookie decorations. Afterward, he felt crummy.

"I thought I'd left them safely out of reach, but when I noticed some were gone, I instantly knew who had taken them," Bulmer told the *Bournemouth Echo*. "Over the years, Marley's been no stranger to eating things he shouldn't, and usually they pass through. But this time he started acting strangely and looked like he was going into shock. He was violently sick and brought up some of the ribbon."

She took Marley to the PDSA pet hospital in Bournemouth where vets had to perform two surgeries, trying to save his life. They removed 34 decorative ribbons that were causing a potentially fatal blockage. They also discovered that the dog had swallowed several bones that had become lodged in his stomach.

"It was a lengthy, high-risk surgery," said senior vet Aoife Clancy. "Marley's chances of surviving the night were looking poor. Thankfully, he pulled through but needed critical round-the-clock care for four days before he could go home.

"It's important that owners make sure decorations and toxic Christmas foods are safe from curious paws, as they can be incredibly harmful to our pets. Foods including mince pies, chocolate, onions, raisins, grapes, macadamia nuts, sage-and-onion stuffing, and Christmas cake can all be fatal."

Marley came close to *meeting his baker.* "There were so many times we thought that was it, and with the heaviest of hearts, we were preparing to say goodbye to him," Bulmer said. "But he kept on fighting, and somehow made it through surgery. He really is our miracle dog."

When Marley was brought home, he was put on "strict cage rest." Said Bulmer at the time, "We've not moved from his side now he's finally at home, and even sleep next to him at night. He's getting better and that's the best Christmas present I could ever want."

BAD HAIR (TIE) DAY

Tiki the black Labrador retriever got her tummy all tied up in knots—literally. During a weird week of gluttony, she consumed 62 hair ties, 8 pairs of undies, and assorted other nonfood items.

Like most Labs, Tiki always had a healthy appetite. She was ready to eat anytime, anywhere—and, apparently, anything. One day in 2015, the family pet of Sara Weiss of Mars, Pennsylvania, began puking and suffering from diarrhea. When the pooch didn't respond to medication, Sara brought her to Good Shepherd's Veterinary Hospital in Mars.

Dr. Hisham Ibrahim—known as Dr. I to his staff—x-rayed her and saw a strange mass in her stomach. Unable to determine what it was, he performed nearly two hours of exploratory surgery. Like a magician pulling a long string of scarves out of a hat, the veterinarian began yanking hair ties out of the dog's tummy.

"I found this hair band attached to another hair band to another one to another one and to other things again," Ibrahim told Pittsburgh television station WTAE.

Emily Cottle, the head vet technician, added, "It was quite an experience to see. Doctor I started pulling handfuls of different items out. Four rubber bands, a Band-Aid, eight pairs of underwear, and 62 hair bands are a lot to be in a dog's stomach, especially of Tiki's size."

Dr. Ibrahim said that what Tiki had eaten "was just amazing." The delicate operation was kind of funny because it left Tiki in stitches. "Thank God, we were able to pull her through, and Tiki recovered very well," the vet told WTAE. A follow-up exam showed that the dog had no further knotty problems.

Tiki had common ties with a cat named Winnie. In 2017, she needed surgery to remove 46 hair ties from her stomach.

Winnie lived with Dewey "DJ" Nowlin and Alicia Brown of Roanoke, Virginia. Over a period of a year, Brown often complained that she was losing hair ties and couldn't figure out why. "It was always kind of a running joke that my girlfriend couldn't find hair ties, and I'm like, well, Winnie probably ate them," Nowlin told local television station WDBJ. Of course, neither one really believed that.

But then they noticed Winnie didn't seem her normal self. She wasn't eating or drinking, so they took her to a local vet. X-rays showed an unidentified foreign object lodged in her stomach. She was then transferred to Animal Emergency and Critical Care in Lynchburg. With a device called an endoscope, Dr. Jay Harper was able to determine that the mass in the cat's stomach was composed of thin hair bands.

"This was the most hair ties I'd ever seen," Dr. Harper told WDBJ. "It's usually one or two or three [that a cat might consume], so we knew it was going to be a bunch. I had guessed twenty to thirty." His estimate was way off.

"After the scoping procedure was finished and all material was removed from the stomach, we cleaned everything off to assess what all was there," the animal clinic posted on Facebook. "The final count was 46 hair ties with some other miscellaneous material. Needless to say, Winnie is feeling much better now."

Said Nowlin, "I was like, 'One day, Winnie, you're going to be on YouTube and be a cat sensation.' This was not the way I wanted her to do it."

Well, at least she made the *mews*.

ABOUT THE AUTHOR

Allan Zullo is the author of more than 120 non-fiction books on subjects ranging from sports and the supernatural to history and animals.

He has written the bestselling Haunted Kids series, published by Scholastic, which is filled with chilling stories based on, or inspired by, documented cases from the files of ghost hunters. Allan also has introduced Scholastic readers to the Ten True Tales series, about people of all ages who have met the challenges of dangerous, sometimes life-threatening, situations.

As an animal lover, he is the author of such books as *The Dog Who Saved Christmas and Other True Animal Tales*, *The Dog Who Saved Halloween and Other True Animal Tales*, *Bad Pets Save Christmas*, *Bad Pets Hall of Shame*, *Bad Pets: Bad to the Bone*, *Bad Pets Most Wanted!*, *Bad Pets on the Loose!*, *Bad Pets: True Tales of Misbehaving Animals*, *Miracle Pets: True Tales of Courage and Survival*, *Incredible Dogs and Their Incredible Tales*, *True Tales of Animal Heroes*, and *Surviving Sharks and Other Dangerous Creatures*.

Allan, the grandfather of five and the father of two grown daughters, lives near Asheville, North Carolina. To learn more about the author, visit his website at www.allanzullo.com.

More pets behaving badly!

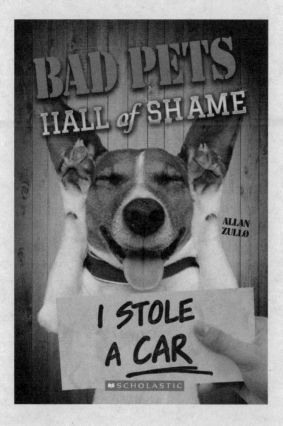

These pets are bad to the bone!